ITALY
IN COLOUR

ITALY
IN COLOUR

CHARLES SCRIBNER'S SONS
NEW YORK

CONTRIBUTORS

Texts by RICCARDO BARSOTTI
MARIA BERNARDINI
RENZO CHIARELLI
RICCARDO GATTESCHI
CARLO GIORDANO
GIOVANNA MAGI
LUIGI NOFERINI
EUGENIO PUCCI
DOMENICO REA

Translation from the Italian by MICHAEL HOLLINGWORTH
Regional maps by OSVALDO MONTELATICI
Editor: MARCO BANTI
Assistant Editor: SIMONETTA GIORGI
Photographs from: the archives of the publishers,
S.E.F., Turin,
Marzari, Schio,
Scala, Florence,
and by courteous permission of the branches of
the Ente Provinciale per il Turismo in Belluno,
Benevento, Brescia, Lucca, Naples, Padua,
Perugia, Salerno, Siena.

ISBN 0-684-14797-1
Library of Congress Catalog Card Number 76-023577

PREFACE

The aim which has led to the planning and publishing of this book is that of offering the public at large a panorama of Italy, this country of ours which can be described, without exaggeration, as magnificent.

We have kept in mind the situation of the traveller of today, who is often forced, despite himself, to make a stereotyped tour of the well-known sights. In this book, alongside photographs of the more famous views or monuments which he has probably seen, he will also find lesser-known attractions — places or buildings which he might well have had the pleasant surprise of discovering for himself, had he not been subject to the terrible tyranny of time.

In order to help the reader to place the monuments and localities described in their geographical context, we have organised the book according to the various regions of Italy, from north to south, each region being accompanied by an explanatory map.

Of course, the book cannot be expected to illustrate the whole of Italy, which would obviously be impossible in a volume of this size. Indeed, in order to include « everything » and avoid hurting anyone's feelings, many volumes would be necessary.

But then it was not our aim to cover « all » Italy. Instead, we have sought to offer the visitor a panoramic view of Italy, or better still, to take him on a « tour » of some of its many natural and man-made beauties.

We believe we have fulfilled this aim.

We think this book will lead those who are already acquainted with our country to a greater appreciation of what it has to offer; and for those who have not yet had that pleasure, here is a perfectly feasible tour in which they can get to know Italy.

INDEX OF PLACES

PIEDMONT
AND *VALLEY OF AOSTA*

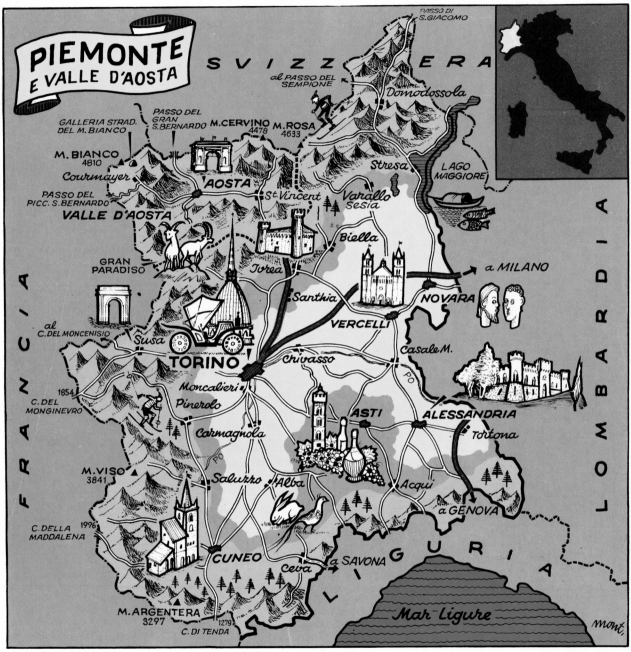

An immense and imposing Alpine range dominating a fertile plain through which flows the largest of Italian rivers, the Po, with all its many tributaries, forms the physical structure of Piedmont. It is also the origin of its name, that is the region « at the foot of the mountains ». The history of Piedmont, as of all northern Italy, is one of domination by successive different powers. Its first inhabitants were the Ligurians, who came here from the coastal regions but their tranquillity was destroyed in the following centuries by a series of invasions by the

Tamini, the Celts, the Salassi, and finally the Romans. Under them, the first important population centres, such as Turin, Ivrea, Asti, Tortona, Acqui and Susa, had their modest beginnings. In the period of Roman domination the region was called Cisalpine Gaul, but with the fall of the Roman Empire it was first invaded by the Longobards, then settled by the Franks under Charlemagne who divided the region into the three « marches » or territories of Turin, Monferrato and Ivrea. The last Marquis of Turin was Olderico Manfredi, who on his death in 1045 left the marquisate to his daughter Adelaide; she in turn married Count Otto of Savoy, son of Humbert Biancamano. Thus opened the long period of Piedmont's history linked to the fortunes of the House of Savoy.

Each ruling power left its imprint in the form of fortresses, castles, buildings and works of art. The Counts of Savoy were jealous guardians of their territories even during the period of the free communes, until finally in 1418 Amedeo VIII brought the entire region under his control; then under Emanuele Filiberto (1528-80) Turin became the seat of the Savoy Court. After the French Revolution, Piedmont fell into the hands of France under Napoleon I, and the Savoy family was forced to withdraw to Sardinia; but they returned in 1815 to reinforce their state by annexing Liguria, and to begin the work of unifying Italy. In 1841 the crown passed to Carlo Alberto who in 1848-49 instigated the first war of Italian independence against Austria, unfortunately with disastrous results. Defeated at the battle of Novara he was forced into exile and was succeeded by his son, Victor Emmanuel II, who had at his side the brilliant diplomat Count Camillo Benso di Cavour. In the following ten years Cavour strengthened the economy, created a strong army and consolidated the state's diplomatic position through an alliance with Napoleon III of France. With French support, Cavour in 1859 renewed the war against Austria and finally defeated her. As a result, Piedmont annexed Emilia, Tuscany and the Kingdom of the Two Sicilies, Victor Emmanuel II assumed the title of King of Italy, and Turin became the capital of the new kingdom until the year 1865.

In the north-west corner of Italy, above Piedmont, is the spectacularly beautiful Valley of Aosta, extending up to the famous Mont Blanc, where Italy's border meets those of France and Switzerland. Scenically one of the most magnificent regions in the whole Alpine chain, the valley is surrounded by high snow-capped peaks, including the Gran San Bernardo and Gran Paradiso.

The origins of the valley's first inhabitants are lost in time; it was dominated by the Salassi tribe until the 2nd century B. C., when conquered by the Romans, who founded Augusta Praetoria, the present-day city of Aosta, where the Arch of Augustus dating from this period is still to be seen. A sturdy Roman road linking Ivrea and Lyons meant economic prosperity for the area, the smallest region of the Italian peninsula. During the Middle Ages, the area was devastated by the Saracens, and was later dominated by various rulers: the Byzantine Empire, the Longobards, the Franks and the Burgundians. Foreign rule gave way to the rise of the feudal lords, until they were in turn curbed by Count Thomas I of Savoy. Many families rose to eminence through their wealth and political astuteness, among them the Challants who left behind a graphic record of their achievements in the striking medieval buildings which they constructed. In 1025 Humbert Biancamano of Savoy became effective ruler of the region and later had bestowed on him the title of Count of Aosta. In 1238 Frederick II elevated the status of the valley to that of a dukedom; in 1416 the Emperor Siegmund granted the Counts of Savoy the title of Dukes of Aosta, and from that moment, apart from a brief period of French domination, they became the real rulers of the valley. In the Second World War, the area was liberated by the partisans, and in 1945 it was formed into a self-governing region.

TURIN

To the discerning traveller who would like to know the whole of Italy from one end to the other — from the Alps to Sicily — Turin is like the beautiful prelude to a vast symphony. Seen from one of the many high points which surround it, the city has an incomparable beauty. Before one's gaze lies a panorama of hills, rivers, mountains, colours and space without equal in the world. To the beauty of a Turin already beautiful much was added by Filippo Juvarra (1676-1736), the Sicilian architect whose works make the panorama even more varied. The city's natural beauties are interwoven and harmonised with those of this masterly artist whose genius has left its indelible stamp on Turin from the time it was a royal capital. There is a refined and gentlemanly air about everything. One feels it in the buildings, the streets and boulevards, and in the

people themselves. But there is nothing weak or effeminate about this refinement; rather it is aristocratic and civilised, the attitude of a people living in a real world and ready to put their hand to any stern task they are called upon to do. It was Turin that assumed the leadership in the wars of Italian independence during the Risorgimento, and it was here that Italian industry first developed on a large scale. Today it is world famous for the cars and aircraft it turns out, it is the centre of the Italian broadcasting and TV system, and it is looked to as a creator of fashion. Despite material progress, however, Turin has managed to preserve what is most beautiful in its heritage mainly because its citizens, with this sense of refinement they possess, are able to keep an eye on the past while living in the present.

The Mole Antonelliana. - Designed by the engineer Alessandro Antonelli (whence its name), this great building has become almost emblematic of Turin's skyline. It was begun in 1863 but not completed until 1897 because of the difficulty of its all-masonry construction. A violent cyclone in 1953 destroyed nearly 150 feet of its spire. The damaged section was replaced by a metal structure, completed in 1961. An elevator takes visitors to the top of the building which has a magnificent view of the city.

Royal Palace. - Built in 1658 on the ruins of San Giovanni Palace by the architect Amadeo di Castellamonte for Carlo Emanuele II. In its luxurious apartments lived the kings of Sardinia and, until 1865, the kings of Italy. On the evening of March 23, 1848, from the balcony of the palace's armoury, Carlo Alberto proclaimed the first war of independence. The rooms on the first floor are magnificently decorated and contain a fine collection of Far Eastern ceramics.

Basilica of Superga. - Standing on the hill of the same name 2000 feet above sea level, it was begun in 1717 by Filippo Juvarra to fulfil a vow made by Vittorio Amadeo II after his victory over the troops of Louis XIV at Turin in 1706, and was completed fourteen years later. Its combination of dome, eight Corinthian columns, two bell-towers and portico has an austere effect. The church, built on a centralized plan, contains valuable reliefs and statues. In the crypt, entrance to which is on the left-hand side of the church, are the tombs of the Savoy kings.

Equestrian monument to Emanuele Filiberto Duke of Savoy. - Turin has many monuments adorning its squares and gardens in memory of deeds and men connected with the city's history. Among the most impressive is this statue, which represents the Duke sheathing his sword after the victorious battle of St. Quentin (1557), the victory which allowed him to regain possession of his dominions. A bronze by the Torinese sculptor Carlo Marocchetti (1805-1867) it stands in the picturesque Piazza San Carlo.

Palazzo Madama. - The most symbolic of Turin's buildings, since it epitomizes a thousand years of the city's history. The imposing structure includes three parts of different origins: the ancient Roman gate from the time of Augustus; the Gothic remains of the 13th-century fortress of the Marquises of Monferrato; and finally the Palazzo Madama, whose facade and double staircase by Filippo Juvarra are among the greatest architectural works of the 18th century. The name « Palazzo Madama » derives from the period towards the end of the 17th century when it was the home of Maria Cristina of France, widow of Amedeo I, known as « Madama Reale ». In its central hall, the Italian Senate held its sittings after Italy's unification, until the capital was transferred from Turin.

Savoy Gallery. - HANS MEMLING (about 1433-1494): Detail of the *Passion of Christ*. One of the most celebrated works of the Flemish master, painted about 1470.

Savoy Gallery. - VAN ORLEY (about 1488-1541): *Consecration of the King of France.* A fine work by the 16th century Flemish painter.

AOSTA

Roman Arch of Augustus - This is one of the major monuments which testify to the Roman origins of Augusta Praetoria, founded in 25 B. C. by Terentius Varro Murena. It was erected to record the Roman victory over the Salassi warriors. The slate roof was added in 1716 by order of the City Council to protect the arch from damage through water seepage.

Bailliage Tower - Standing at the north-east corner of the ancient Roman wall, and formerly known as the Palatian Tower from the name of the Lords Palais who built it in the 12th century. Later it became the seat of the Podestà of Aosta (or Bailiff), from 1265 to 1537, from which its modern name derives. Later still it served as a courthouse and prison.

Fenis Castle. - Standing about 20 kilometres outside Aosta, this ancient building, if not the most beautiful, is certainly the most picturesque among the many castles to be seen in the valley. It was already standing on this spot in 1242, but owes its present appearance to the powerful Challant family. It was Aimon de Challant who built its towers and battlements between 1340 and 1350. The castle was acquired in 1895 by the architect Alfredo d'Andrade, who restored it and donated it to the State. At present it houses the Valley of Aosta Museum of Furniture and Furnishings.

GRESSONEY. - Among the many local costumes that are still worn in the Valley of Aosta, these which belong to the Valley of Gressoney are the most famous. The red skirt, the white lace blouse and, above all, the bonnet woven with golden thread make such a charming ensemble that even some of the holiday-makers imitate the dress of the locals and wear their costume on festive days.

THE MONT BLANC GROUP. - The « Grand Capucin » and « Trident » peaks. This photograph admirably captures the region's Alpine splendours. Huge granite masses, thrusting upward into towering spires and sharpened by the erosion of the elements, they stand out imposingly against the sky.

CLIMBING THE CRESTA DI VERRA. - This peak lies to the south-west of the Monte Rosa group. On the right, the summit of the Gran Tourmalin towers above the Val Tournanches. In the background, the great snow-covered mass of the Gran Paradiso.

LOMBARDY

A rich mountainous zone with lakes, rivers and canals, and the immense fertile plain of the Po River are the distinguishing features of the region of Lombardy. Its origins are lost in prehistoric times, from the Stone and Bronze Ages, the Iron Age and establish-ment of the first civilisations, up until the invasions of the Gauls who settled there alongside the Umbrians and Etruscans. The Gauls proved stubborn adversaries of the Roman legions, but were forced finally to yield and assimilate the new Roman culture, which brought economic prosperity and civilisation to Lombardy. After the advent of Christianity, the region played a major role during the time of St. Ambrose, Bishop of Milan from 374 to 397. But the decline of the western half of the divided Roman Empire, torn by struggles between Odoacer, Goths and Byzantines, opened the way for the disastrous barbarian invasions. For two centuries the Longobards occupied the region, establishing their court there: they gave it the name of « Longobardia », which has since become « Lombardia » (Lombardy). The Longobards were succeeded by the Franks, led by Charlemagne, and the people of Lombardy came under the rule of the political and social system of feudalism. But the year 888 introduced a period of anarchy in which the feudal lords seized power in their own hands and were opposed by the increasingly powerful Church leaders. The task of putting things in order fell to the German emperor Otto I, who in 961 had himself crowned King of Italy at Milan. Lombardy thus became part of the German empire with the same form of government, which led to the supremacy of the count-bishops and the formation of a new aristocracy. This in turn gave way to the age of the free communes in the cities. Milan, Como, Lodi, Cremona, Bergamo, Brescia and Pavia fought for their independence from the Empire, and when Frederick I, known as Barbarossa from his red beard, tried to oppose them, they formed a league and defeated him at the famous battle of Legnano (1176). After gaining their freedom the Communes were torn by internal strife among the different social classes, and their decline resulted in a new form of government — the « Signoria » — composed of the wealthy families who were shrewd enough to seize power, like the Visconti and Sforzas in Milan and the Gonzagas in Mantua. The long struggle between France and Spain for the possession of Italy which marked the first half of the 16th century ended finally with the defeat of the French at St. Quentin (1557). As a result of the peace treaty Milan became part of the Spanish dominions and remained so for more than 150 years. Spanish misgovernment was such that it came as a relief when Austria, having won the War of the Spanish Succession (1702-13), took the place of Spain. Austrian administration proved wise on the whole and tended to promote the well-being of the region.

The French Revolution and the military genius of Napoleon meant another change of masters for Lombardy. It became an integral part of the French Empire, and the people assimilated the social and political ideals of the Revolution; the result was a growing sentiment of national awareness among the population and a strong desire to see Italy united and independent. When Napoleon was defeated at Waterloo in 1815 and Lombardy was handed back to Austria, the social and political situation was so changed that the ruling interests of the Austrian Empire met with powerful opposition. Austrian repression sparked off the heroic era of the Italian Risorgimento when Milan, Mantua, and Brescia rebelled against their foreign overlords. The wars of Italian independence led by Piedmont against Austria ended in final victory, and Lombardy in 1859 became part of the young Italian kingdom to play an essential part in the subsequent growth of the Italian nation.

MILAN

There is a widespread but mistaken idea that Milan is inferior in beauty to other Italian cities. To refute this judgment it should be enough to quote the example of so famous a person as the French writer Stendhal whose love for Milan was so strong that he made it his adopted home and went so far as to describe himself as « Milanese » in his epitaph. Milan is no place for a hasty visit. Like a coy and bashful lady, it refuses to reveal all its charms at once. Its fascination must be discovered little by little. It is alive, not a dead museum. It hasn't the time to stand admiring itself. But there is a vital link between present and past, and though an industrial city it has not rejected its former splendours. There is no gap to be found in its artistic evolution which extends from Roman times to our own day and in which all the different styles are represented. It is enough to look at its most famous buildings: the colonnade at San Lorenzo, Sant'Ambrogio, the Cathedral, Piazza dei Mercanti, Sforza Castle, Santa Maria delle Grazie, San Satiro, San Carlo al Corso, La Scala Theatre, the Arch of Peace in the Parisian style, the Pirelli skyscraper,

the Velasca Tower. Then there are its museums and art galleries such as the Brera, Sforza Castle, the Poldi-Pezzoli, in which are housed masterpieces by Mantegna, Caravaggio, Michelangelo, Raphael, Piero della Francesca to mention only a few. Add to these the Museum of Technology and Science dedicated to the great Leonardo da Vinci. And there are the numerous galleries where contemporary art has pride of place. It is superfluous to go into detail about Milan's musical life: enough to mention La Scala and Casa Ricordi. The cultural environment is stimulating and among the most active in Italy or in Europe. The « Piccolo Teatro » (Little Theatre) has made a major contribution for more than 20 years to the understanding of plays dealing with the problems of our time. Such is Milan which, overtopped by the statue of Our Lady on the highest point of the Cathedral (the « Madonnina ») welcomes every visitor, Italian or foreigner, with equal warmth. A city which can offer love, in its quiet way, especially if you are one who can see how much beauty is hidden under its mists.

The Cathedral. - The most important example of Gothic architecture in Italy, it was begun by order of Gian Galeazzo Visconti in 1386 and completed in 1813. Artists from many countries worked on it over the centuries. Its 135 spires (on the highest of which, at 330 ft., stands the « Madonnina »), 2245 statues and innumerable pinnacles make it an unforgettable sight. Its most impressive part is the polygonal apse with its three stained-glass windows, created by Filippino degli Organi in 1389.

Gallery of Victor Emmanuel II. - Designed by the architect Giuseppe Mengoni (1829-77), it links the Cathedral square and La Scala. Thronged with people until late at night, it is called the « salotto » (drawing-room) by the Milanese because of its elegant shops, cafés and restaurants.

La Scala Theatre. - The most famous opera house in the world. Neo-classical in style, it was built by G. Piermarini in 1776-78 on the former site of the 14th-century church of Santa Maria della Scala: hence its name.

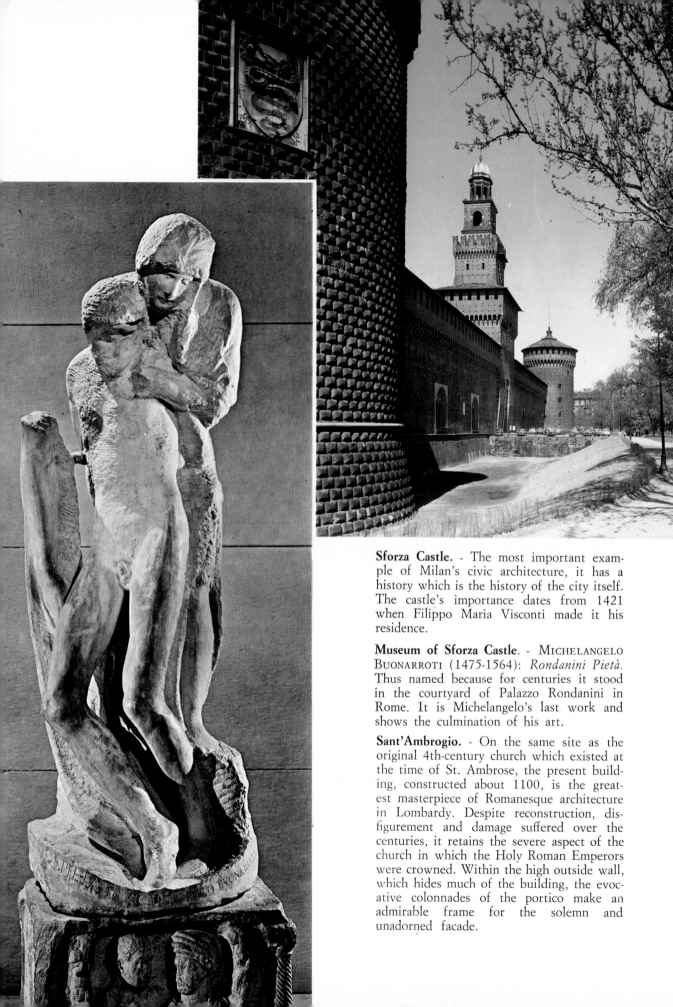

Sforza Castle. - The most important example of Milan's civic architecture, it has a history which is the history of the city itself. The castle's importance dates from 1421 when Filippo Maria Visconti made it his residence.

Museum of Sforza Castle. - MICHELANGELO BUONARROTI (1475-1564): *Rondanini Pietà.* Thus named because for centuries it stood in the courtyard of Palazzo Rondanini in Rome. It is Michelangelo's last work and shows the culmination of his art.

Sant'Ambrogio. - On the same site as the original 4th-century church which existed at the time of St. Ambrose, the present building, constructed about 1100, is the greatest masterpiece of Romanesque architecture in Lombardy. Despite reconstruction, disfigurement and damage suffered over the centuries, it retains the severe aspect of the church in which the Holy Roman Emperors were crowned. Within the high outside wall, which hides much of the building, the evocative colonnades of the portico make an admirable frame for the solemn and unadorned facade.

Brera Gallery. - RAPHAEL (1483-1520): *Espousal of the Virgin.*

Brera Gallery. - PIERO DELLA FRANCESCA (about 1420-1492): *Madonna and Child, with Angels, Saints and Federico da Montefeltro, Duke of Urbino.*

Santa Maria delle Grazie, Refectory. - LEONARDO DA VINCI (1452-1519): *Last Supper.* There are few works of art in the world as famous as this one, due both to the many stories about it and its unusual history. It took Leonardo two years to paint it, but according to contemporary reports there were frequent interruptions in the work.

The technique used was unusual, and unfortunately so imperfect that the fresco began to deteriorate immediately and rapidly. Vasari, hardly sixty years later, was able to see only « a dazzling stain ». There have been many attempts to restore the work, but these may well have served mainly to worsen the situation. The last careful attempt at restoration was in recent years, after the fresco had miraculously survived the bombing which almost completely destroyed the refectory in 1943.

Despite the disastrous and unavoidable deterioration, which has reduced the work almost to a shadow of its former self, it still retains its original fascination, and before such a masterpiece one can only agree with the great art critic Berenson that Leonardo « touched nothing without transforming it into eternal beauty ».

Santa Maria delle Grazie, Refectory. - LEONARDO DA VINCI (1452-1519): *Last Supper*. The Redeemer (detail).

29

PAVIA

The Certosa. - Four centuries of Italian art are epitomized in this famous and most beautiful of Carthusian monasteries. Masterpieces of sculpture, invaluable paintings, exquisite stained-glass, wood carvings, wrought iron and bronze are all to be found in rare harmony within the superb construction of its walls. Founded in 1396 by Gian Galeazzo Visconti, repeated delays meant that work was not finished until the completion of the facade in 1560.

Visconti Castle. - This imposing rectangular-shaped building, of brick construction, was begun by Galleazzo II Visconti immediately after his conquest of the city (1351). Its construction was almost certainly directed by Bernardo da Venezia, and the Venetian influence is evident. Residence of the Visconti family, it was adorned with valuable paintings which since then have unfortunately been lost. Towards the middle of the 15th century the castle passed into the hands of the Sforzas, and reached the height of its splendour. With the death of Francesco Maria Sforza and the end of his family's rule, the building fell into disrepair. For centuries it served as a military barracks and each foreign power left its destructive imprint on it. Especially serious was the damage caused by Lautrec's French troops in 1527 when an entire wing was destroyed. Following considerable restoration work begun in 1921, the castle has been used to house various collections from the city's museums.

Covered bridge. - A reconstruction of the ancient bridge destroyed during hostilities in 1944, it is the most typical sight along the city's waterways.

COMO. - The city, whose origins are said to go back to the Palafitte and Bronze Ages, is a modern and important industrial centre. On the shores of the famous lake and surrounded by tall hills covered with luxuriant vegetation, it is also an important tourist resort.

MADERNO DEL GARDA. - A splendid tourist centre lying on a picturesque part of the lake. Of Roman origin, it was the summer seat of the Gonzagas when they ruled Mantua.

SIRMIONE ON LAKE GARDA. - Now a well-known resort, there were villas and thermal baths here in Roman times. The Latin poet Catullus sang its charms in immortal verse. Pictured in the photograph is Scaliger Castle, completely surrounded by the lake, built by Mastino I in 1259.

LAKE HYDRA. - An enchanting view of this lake in the Sabbia Valley.

BRESCIA

The Loggia. - Brescia's most remarkable public building and an admirable example of Renaissance creativity. Its construction was begun in 1492, suspended in 1508 and resumed a few years later to be completed in 1574. The lower part, with its open portico and wide arches, is the work of Tommasino Formentone, of Vicenza. The upper part, with its splendidly decorated pilaster strips, frieze and large rectangular windows, was designed by Iacopo Sansovino. Other contributions to the building also came from Palladio, Alessi and Rusconi.

Capitolium. - The Capitoline Temple was excavated in 1823 at the foot of the Cidneo Hill. It was built by the Emperor Vespasian in 73 A.D. in memory of his victory over the army of the Emperor Vitellius. Standing on elevated ground facing the forum, it was reached from the latter by a stairway which has been reconstructed. The vestibule, 40 yards long, included 16 Corinthian columns some of which are still to be seen. Its three doorways give access to the temple's chambers, probably dedicated to Jove, Minerva and Juno, and thence to the rooms of the Archeological Museum.

Civic Museum of Christian and Modern Art. - *The Cross of Desiderius, or of Galla Placidia.* This precious work of the Ravenna goldsmiths is encrusted with gems and cameos. Executed in gilded silver foil, at the centre it has a medallion bearing a relief figure of Christ the Redeemer. Worth noting on the lower arm is the medallion on gilded glass depicting a family group. It is known as the Cross of Desiderius because it was donated by the king of that name to the Benedictine monastery of San Michele.

Winged Victory. - This magnificent bronze statue, originally gilded, is the most famous work in the Roman Museum. It was discovered in 1826 in the space between the Capitoline Temple and the rock-face behind it. Opinions about the statue vary, but according to the most likely theory it was part of a group which adorned the pediment of the temple. The goddess, held by some to be a copy of an original by Praxiteles, is depicted in the act of stepping into a chariot. In fact, the remains of the chariot and horses were found at the same time.

Pinacoteca Civica Tosio-Martinengo. - Raphael [Raffaello Sanzio] (1483-1520):
Angel.

VENETIA AND FRIULI VENEZIA GIULIA

The varied scenery and the special natural beauties of Venetia have made it dear to Italians and foreigners alike. Its mountain structure (which includes part of the Western Alps, the Tridentine Alps, the Lessine mountains, the Asiago plateau, the Dolomites and part of the Carnic Alps) slopes gently down to the Venetian plain. Here, in the provinces of Belluno, Padua, Rovigo, Treviso, Venice, Verona and Vicenza, there is evidence of activity in every field of human life, political and military, religious, commercial and industrial, not to mention the rich artistic heritage created here over the centuries. The region's mountains and watercourses were also the scene of courageous exploits during the wars of Italian independence and the First World War.

The first inhabitants in Venetia's history were the Euganei, who settled in the region of the Lessine mountains, and the Euganean hills. They were followed by the Carni and then the Veneti who proved from the first extremely able sailors. The Veneti were threatened by the expansionism of the Gauls, but the latter were held in check by the military force of Rome.

The region drew considerable benefit from its alliance with Rome, not only from the point of view of security but also in its expanding trade. When the Roman Empire dissolved, however, Venetia fell prey to the barbarians who descended from the north, eager to conquer the fertile lands of the Italian peninsula. The havoc created by the barbarian tribes, their rapacity and ferociousness forced the Venetians to seek refuge in the lagoon, thus giving birth to the city of Venice.

The other cities on the mainland went through a long gloomy period of decline during the barbarian invasions, but revived with the advent of the free communes and regained their liberty in the 12th century through the Veronese League between Verona, Vicenza, Padua and Venice. The alliance was successful against the emperor Frederick Barbarossa whose armies were unable to defeat the better organised troops of the League.

Ruling power in the Italian cities later passed from the Commune to the « Signoria », an oligarchy of prominent families, leading to a period of fierce internal struggles for power and clashes between opposing cities with expansionist aims. This state of affairs was resolved by the growing power of Venice which, strongly established in the Adriatic, now turned its attention to the conquest of the Venetian region, and in a brief space of time during the 15th century succeeded in creating a strong, unified state. Venice's dominion over the surrounding country, however, provoked envious reaction among the European powers who, in 1529, formed the League of Cambrai and attempted to break up the new political and military entity. But Venice was strong enough to resist this aggression, and destroyed the League's unity through diplomacy and force of arms, so that gradually it was obliged to renounce its aims.

In 1571 the Venetian Republic proved the determining factor in the defeat of the Turks at Lepanto. Venice's supremacy over the Venetian region lasted for some four centuries, and contributed enormously to the city's prosperity, until in 1797 it was conquered by Napoleon I. It fell under the dominion of Austria which, except for French rule between 1805 and 1815, held Venetia until 1866 when it became part of the Kingdom of Italy. The frontier established at this stage was rather unfavourable to Italy, and it was only after the defeat of Austria in the First World War that adjustments were made and the Austrians finally forced to withdraw completely.

Very similar to Venetia, in its pleasant countryside with watercourses crossing fertile plains, is the adjacent region of Friuli-Venezia Giulia, where so many Italian soldiers lost their lives fighting in the First World War. The mountain passes of this northern region served as the gateway to Italy during the barbarian invasions. The centres of its four present-day provinces are the cities of Gorizia, Udine, Trieste and Pordenone. In ancient times, the region was inhabited by Ligurians and Celts; later came the Romans, who in 181 B. C. founded Aquileia. The city was then on the shores of the Adriatic but has since been cut off from the sea by deposits of silt from the Isonzo and Tagliamento rivers. As the Roman Empire collapsed, the Visigoths, Huns, Ostrogoths and Slavs invaded the region, and in 568 the Longobards, led by their king Alboinus, overcame the token resistance of the Romans based in Aquileia and established themselves here. The Longobard capital, on the present-day site of Cividale, was called « Forum Julii », from which the Friuli plain derives its name. After a period of struggle with the Papacy, the Longobard kingdom was conquered by the Franks who became rulers of this region. They retained its capital but renamed it « Civitas Austriae ». In 915 the region was united by the emperor Otto I to the dukedom of Bavaria.

The policy followed by later German emperors was one of support for the powerful bishops against the rebellious feudal lords; especially favoured was the Bishop of Aquileia whose control of the region continued until 1420. In this year Venice, which had gained increasing power, succeeded after a period of struggle in imposing its rule on the region of Friuli. The Venetian Republic's conquest was partly motivated by its loss during the preceding century of the Istrian peninsula and Trieste. In fact, in 1382 Trieste had put itself under the Austrian Empire of the Hapsburgs, who retained virtual control of the city until 1918. From the time of the Venetian conquest until 1515 there were continual wars, caused first by the invasions of the Turks and then by a dispute between Venice and the Hapsburgs over the feudal holding of Gorizia; but political control of the region remained substantially unchanged by the wars. Venice retained control of most of the Friuli plain and the Istrian coast closer to Venice, including the town of Monfalcone; Austria controlled the Isonzo valley, the counties of Gorizia, Gradisca and Istria, and Trieste. This situation remained more or less stable until the end of the 18th century, although the obvious clash of interests between the two powers caused many minor incidents. The development of Trieste as a major port took place during this period, and in fact its facilities were expanded virtually to the stage at which they remain today: of great importance as an outlet for the Austrian Empire, the port became the largest in the Adriatic. Venetian rule came to an end in 1797 when Napoleon transferred control of Friuli to Austria; it remained under Austrian rule, except for a brief period, until 1866. Then during the Italian Risorgimento the people of Friuli rebelled against their Austrian rulers, and after the third Italian war of independence the western part of the region was united to the Kingdom of Italy. Trieste and Gorizia, however, were still in the hands of the Hapsburgs, and it was not until the 1914-18 war that they became finally Italian.

The region had to face many problems in the aftermath of the Great War. Confusion was caused by competing claims between different groups adhering more strongly either to Italy or Austria. Partisans fought against the Germans here as in other regions of Italy during the Second World War, but the struggle was complicated by divergent political and national allegiancies. The partisan war had its climax in a popular uprising which saved most of the region's industrial installations from destruction by the Germans. Shortly afterwards, however, Yugoslav troops arrived in Trieste and a period of serious unrest and violence followed.

An Allied government, set up to counteract Yugoslav claims, controlled the area until 1954, when, as a result of the London Agreement, Trieste became once more part of Italy. However, Italy lost a considerable amount of territory in the provinces of Gorizia and Trieste to Yugoslavia.

VENICE

This incomparable city is unique in the world not only for its great beauty, but for its peculiar structure. It seems to recount at every step, in a language of its own, its long history, begun during the decay of the Roman Empire and the barbarian invasions.

By their destruction of the towns in the region, the barbarians forced the inhabitants to seek refuge on the numerous little islands of Venice's lagoon. And thus the refugees from Aquileia, Altino and Padua settled on the Rialto, and began digging the complex network of canals which holds together the island's foundations. It was this huge project, carried out according to an overall plan, which gave form and substance to the imposing Grand Canal and the innumerable smaller canals of the city which link the city's 118 islands by means of more than 400 bridges. Huge piles cut from tree trunks were installed to fortify the island base and make possible the construction of the houses, buildings and churches which provide the clearest evidence of Venice's former might, achieved through sea trade

and territorial conquest. The Venetians defended their conquered territories by diplomacy and military action whenever necessary for the survival of the Republic.

The present city has been built up over the centuries into a genuine masterpiece of man's intelligence and industry. It is a city which must be seen, because the most brilliant description cannot give a real impression of it. Only by knowing it at first hand, by discovering its canals and squares and its windings alleys, can one understand why it has been described as one of the wonders of the world.

To Venice's unique physical structure must be added the genius of its innumerable artists who alongside its natural beauty have created a myriad of greater or lesser masterpieces of architecture, sculpture and painting. All this makes Venice the goal of artists, writers, poets, scholars and men of culture. Without knowing Venice one cannot claim really to know the complex splendour of Italy's artistic and cultural history.

St. Mark's Cathedral. - This building summarizes almost the entire political, social and religious history of the Venetian Republic. Its origins date back to 829 when the Doge Giustiniano Partecipazio had it built to house the remains of the city's patron saint, St. Mark the Evangelist. In 927 it was destroyed by fire, and it was rebuilt in its present form by the Doge Domenico Contarini between 1043 and 1071. Its plan in the form of a Greek cross and its domes were modelled on those of a Byzantine church, but translated into the Romanesque style. Its original unadorned simplicity was soon covered by beautiful mosaics in precious marbles and architectural decorations of Eastern inspiration, so that it now includes Byzantine, Gothic, Arabic and Renaissance styles. Thus the great Golden Cathedral stands as a complex artistic masterpiece created by illustrious artists and by Venice's capable craftsmen.

St. Mark's Cathedral. Interior. - The magnificent interior of the Cathedral has retained the Byzantine architectural structure dating back to the time of the Doge Contarini: a centralised plan in the form of a Greek cross, with huge main nave and elevated presbytery, and the minor naves in the arms of the cross divided by pillars and columns which sustain the upper galleries. Round arches, resting on square pillars, form a solid support for the five domes. The walls and pillars were originally without their marble covering, which was begun in 1159 with various precious materials, brought mostly from churches and other buildings in the Orient and Dalmatia.

The spellbound awe which one feels inside the cathedral is largely due to the immense mosaic narrative which covers the walls, vaults and domes and has a surface of more than 4.000 square metres. The beginning of this fantastic cycle of pictures dates back to the 11th century and the era of Domenico Selvo, Doge of the Republic from 1071 until 1084. There was a second phase in the 12th and 13th centuries when after an apprentice period the Venetian School had developed its own architectural style from Romanesque. A further stage was reached in the 14th century when the mosaics took their inspiration from the great Venetian school of painting. The splendid pavement, with its varied geometrical designs and animal figures, is a beautiful example of the mosaic art dating from the 12th century.

St. Mark's Square. - The enormous open-air rendezvous of the Venetians. Today as in the past, it is the centre the political, social and religious life of the city. In the harmonious setting of the square are reminders of all the great events in the Republic's glorious history. Centuries ago the square was important because its surface was more solid than other parts of the city. A canal ran through it and it was surrounded by trees.

St. Mark's Square. - On the left the Procuratorie Nuove (residence of the Procurators of St. Mark), a classic work by Vincenzo Scamozzi (1584), which is matched on the right by the Procuratorie Vecchie, built between 1400 and 1500 and probably designed by Mauro Cadussi. At the end of the square, the Napoleonic wing in the neo-classical style by Giuseppe Soli (1807).

The Palace of the Doges. - This magnificent, imposing structure was the residence from as far back as the 9th century of the Doge, Venice's supreme head of state. It was begun at the time of the Doges Angelo and Giustiniano Partecipazio. Destroyed by fire, it was built in its present form, among the highest expressions of Gothic art, in 1340. The architect is unknown, but the stonemason Filippo Calendario and the overseers Pietro and Enrico Baseio were among its builders. Besides Florentine and Milanese artists, the famous Venetian family of marble-workers, the Bons, had a hand in its decoration. The large arches form a base for the graceful loggia which runs along two sides and supports in turn the luminous facade, with its polychrome, lozenge-shaped pattern, divided by the high windows and central balcony. Crowning the stupendous building are the white battlements, giving the whole structure the intricate beauty of a lace embroidery.

Palace of the Doges. Porta della Carta. - Called the Paper Gate because it was the area of the scribes, who compiled documents for presentation in the city's public offices. The elegant structure, in the « international » Gothic style, was built by Giovanni and Bartolomeo Bon in 1438. The figures of the « Virtues » in the niches of the columns are particularly beautiful. At the top is the statue of Justice, below it a tondo with a bust of St. Mark the Evangelist. Over the portal is a sculpture of the « Doge Francesco Foscari and Winged Lion » by L. Ferrari (1885) which has taken the place of a similar work destroyed in 1797.

Palace of the Doges. The courtyard. - In the centre the two bronze well-curbs, the first by Niccolò dei Conti (1556), the second by Alphonso Alberghetti (1559). On the right, the great facade, the lower part in Gothic and the upper in Renaissance style, by Antonio Rizzo (1483-98). In the background on the left, the Baroque-style facade with its clock by Bartolomeo Manopola (1614).

Palace of the Doges. Senate Room. - Here the Doge presided over the sittings of the Senate. The cycle of paintings on the walls and ceiling celebrated divine favours granted to the Republic. The hall was reconstructed by Antonio da Ponte. On the magnificent ceiling, decorated with gilt inlays by Cristoforo Sorte, is Tintoretto's great painting « The Triumph of Venice with Mythological Figures », lying between the oval paintings of T. Dolabella. On the wall behind the throne is « The Doge's Adoration of the Dead Christ », by Jacopo Tintoretto, on the left-hand wall the « Allegory of the League of Cambrai against Venice » and the « Celebration of the Doge Pasquale Cicogna », both by Jacopo Palma the Younger.

Palace of the Doges. Sala del Collegio. - So called because it was the meeting-place of the « College » formed of the leading citizens of the Republic and presided over by the Doge. The College deliberated affairs of state here and gave audience to ambassadors. Its architectural design is by Palladio (1573). On the magnificent ceiling are masterpieces by Paolo Veronese. Among the paintings on the walls (from left to right in the photo): « The Victory of Lepanto », by Paolo Veronese; the « Mystical Nuptials of St. Catherine », by Domenico Tintoretto, and « The Doge Niccolò da Ponte invokes the Virgin », by Jacopo Tintoretto.

Palace of the Doges. Chamber of the Great Council. - The supreme body which held power in Venice met in this chamber. Destroyed by fire in 1577, it was reconstructed by Antonio da Ponte and decorated with subjects suggested by the Florentine scholar Girolamo de' Bardi and the Venetian historian F. Sansovino. Its paintings celebrate the glories of the Republic. Above the platform is Domenico Tintoretto's fine « Paradise », and in the huge rectangle on the ceiling is « Venice among the Gods receiving homage from her subject peoples », by Jacopo Tintoretto.

Bridge of Sighs. - This graceful Baroque structure, by Antonio Contino (1599), spans the Palace Canal, linking the Palace of the Doges and the Prisons. Prisoners passed across the bridge to appear before the judges, and since their only chance to catch a glimpse of the Lagoon was through its open-work windows, they would sigh here, it is said, for their lost freedom.

Palace of the Doges. Stanza degli Scudieri. - TIEPOLO (1696-1770): *Neptune offering Venice the Gifts of the Sea.*

Grand Canal. - This enchanting S-shaped waterway, Venice's aquatic main road, divides the city in two. The splendid dwellings of the oldest noble Venetian families look out onto its waters.

Ca' d'oro. - Built in the fanciful 15th century Venetian style, it derives its name (« House of Gold ») from the gilding which once adorned its facade. Designed by Bartolomeo Bon and Matteo Raverti for the nobleman Marin Contarini, it later passed into the hands of Baron Giorgio Franchetti, who presented the building to the State in 1916, along with the art collection called after him.

Rialto Bridge. - This daring, single-arch design by Antonio da Ponte, who built the bridge between 1588 and 1591, was chosen by the Republic ahead of designs submitted by Palladio and Michelangelo.
The bridge is 150 ft. long, 66 ft. wide, 28 ft. high and supported by 6000 piles at each end.

Ca' Foscari. - The finest example of Venetian Gothic architecture, this building owes its construction to the Doge Francesco Foscari who directed the Republic's political and social life for more than 30 years. It was made famous by its illustrious guests, and above all by the visit of King Henry III of France in 1574. At present it is occupied by the University Institute of Economics and Commerce.

Academy Galleries. - The Academy of Painters and Sculptors was founded in 1750. Officially recognised during the period when its president was Tiepolo, it collected pieces of sculpture and paintings by its members. These formed the first nucleus of the Galleries, though works from many sources were added later. The name « Galleries » instead of « Gallery » derives from the fact that there were originally two collections: one of paintings, the other of statues. Although the statues have now gone, the plural name « Galleries » remained because it was already so well known. The collection includes the best Venetian painting from the 14th to the 18th centuries.

Academy Galleries. - ANDREA MANTEGNA (1431-1506): *St. George.*

Academy Galleries. - GIOVANNI BELLINI (1426-1515): *Madonna of the Saplings.*

Academy Galleries. -Giovanni Bellini (1426-1515): *Madonna with St. John the Baptist.*

Academy Galleries. -Giovanni Bellini (1426 - 1515): *Pietà.*

Academy Galleries. - Vittore Carpaccio (about 1455-1525): *Arrival of the Ambassadors.* Detail. This painting is part of the cycle of the Stories of St. Ursula.

S. Giovanni e Paolo. - A fine example of Venetian Gothic architecture, dedicated to SS. John and Paul, standing in the square of the same name. Begun in 1246 and completed in 1430, it is the Pantheon of the glories of Venice, containing the tombs of citizens given official recognition by the Republic. Its brick facade is incomplete, but the handsome portal displays a remarkable fusion of Gothic and Renaissance elements. It is attributed to Antonio Gambello.

Square of S. Giovanni e Paolo. - ANDREA DEL VERROCCHIO (1435-1488): *Monument to Bartolomeo Colleoni.* This masterpiece by the Florentine sculptor was executed by the Venetian foundryman and sculptor Alessandro Leopardi, who also made the finely-adorned base.

Santa Maria della Salute. - Baroque masterpiece by Baldassare Longhena, on the right of the Grand Canal near St. Mark's Square. The church was built following a decree by the Venetian Senate on October 22, 1630, to offer thanks to the Virgin Mary for having stopped the plague which claimed 47 thousand victims, whence its name of St. Mary of Good Health.

Santa Maria Gloriosa dei Frari. - In the district of San Polo, this church is the most important building in the Venetian Gothic style after St. Mark's. It was built for the Order of the Friars Minor between 1340 and 1443. Its architect seems to have been Fra Scipione Bon. Like S. Giovanni e Paolo, it contains the tombs of illustrious citizens of the Republic, besides numerous artistic master-pieces. The austere facade is divided by pilaster strips and columns; over its doorway are « Christ's Benediction », by Alessandro Vittoria, and the « Madonna and St. Francis », by Bartolomeo Bon.

Santa Maria Gloriosa dei Frari. - TITIAN (about 1477-1576): *The Assumption.*

PADUA

The name of a city is often closely linked with a famous event, an important building in it, or the place where it is situated. For Padua this means St. Anthony — known to the world as St. Anthony of Padua but simply called « the Saint » by the Paduans themselves — who is buried in the great Basilica erected in his honour, and its ancient University, one of the first in Europe, dating from the 13th century. But though less well known, perhaps of greater importance is Padua's artistic heritage. Lying in the tranquil Venetian plain, the city is inhabited by a gentle-mannered but firm-minded people, of the same race as those who fled from the barbarian invasions to found an island home in Venice, and who are tolerant and understanding because they love life. It possesses numerous treasures of art which are a witness to the predominant position it once held in the surrounding country. The height of its splendour was reached in the 14th and early 15th centuries when, under the rule of the Car-

rara family, it offered hospitality to illustrious figures in the world of literature, such as Dante and Petrarch, and of art, such as Giotto, Niccolò Pisano, Filippo Lippi and Donatello. The new ideas inspired by the Renaissance found a fertile soil and the foundations were laid for the school of painting which was to find its highest expression in Mantegna.

Padua is a city in which the past has not completely disappeared, even though the signs of the economic progress which is making it a leading commercial centre are only too evident. It has to be discovered. One need only turn aside from its main thoroughfares and thread one's way through the narrow winding side streets, especially around the Cathedral, to find Renaissance and 16th century Padua, just as in spite of the profound changes in this modern age, a certain traditional atmosphere is still alive at Petrocchi, the café in the centre which remains today the meeting place for those interested in art and culture.

Basilica of St. Anthony. - Erected between
1232 and 1307 by the Franciscans to house
the tomb of St. Anthony. A graceful loggia
adds beauty to the imposing Gothic arches
of the façade, and the eight domes and two
slim towers give the building an almost
Oriental appearance. Inside, the church is
divided into three naves with galleries originally reserved for women. Worthy of note
are the tomb of Gattamelata, by B. Bel-
lano (15th century), the frescoes by Alti-
chiero and Avanzo (1337), and bronzes by
Donatello and assistants.

Equestrian monument to Gattamelata. - This
masterpiece by Donatello (1386-1466), executed in 1453, stands in front of the Basilica. It immortalises Erasmo da Narni (1370-
1443), known as Gattamelata, a courageous
military captain in the service of Venice,
who died in Padua.

Scrovegni Chapel. - GIOTTO (1267-1337): *Flight into Egypt.*

Scrovegni Chapel. - Enrico Scrovegni had the chapel built in 1305, and to paint its frescoes commissioned Giotto, the most celebrated artist of the time. Its brick exterior is in the Romano-Gothic style. The interior, a single rectangular nave with barrel vault ceiling, seems as if designed on purpose to exhibit Giotto's works, so measured and unadorned is its architecture. On the walls are Giotto's paintings of scenes from the lives of Jesus and Mary, the Passion and Ascension and Pentecost. On the entrance wall (shown at right) is his Last Judgement, and on the imitation marble plinth the « Virtues » and « Vices ». Giotto painted the frescoes between 1305 and 1306, and along with those at Assisi they represent the height of his art.

VERONA

Anyone who visits Verona must come away in love with it. No writer or poet from ancient to modern times who has known the city has failed to pay tribute to its charm. Painters have been equally enthusiastic: the singular configuration of its site with its river and hills, and the striking colour tones of the city have furnished them with incomparable material, while the landscape around has won their admiration.

Why such warmth? Charles Dickens described it as « loveable Verona ». And its secret lies in this: Verona is not only beautiful, but loveable; the city is cordial and its people are affable, good-humoured and witty. Situated on the banks of the Adige in the Venetian plain, it was for centuries the « gateway to Italy », and witnessed the migration of entire peoples and the invasions of barbarian kings. After having been a flourishing Roman colony, it was the capital of various kingdoms and decisive battles were fought around it. Within its walls, Alboin died by the hand of Ro-

samund; Theodoric resided here at length; Desiderius, king of the Longobards, made it his last bastion against the Franks of Charlemagne; Berengarius, the first to proclaim himself king of Italy, was killed here; as a free Commune, it was an aggressive member of the Lombard League; it reached its greatest splendour under the Scaliger family, before becoming subject to the Venetian Republic to which it long remained faithful. With these origins and history, Verona is a unique city: unique in that it is consistent yet different in every part. A city of river and hills, of plain with nearby mountains; a city that has been Roman, barbarian, feudal, Renaissance, Baroque and neo-classical, languid and sentimental when it chooses, stern and military the next moment, classical and romantic, and today even boldly modern. Not that it can be identified with any of these; rather, the almost endless series of its component parts makes it a perfect kaleidoscope of unity and diversity.

San Zeno. - The church of San Zeno, built about 1120, is rightly considered Verona's most famous monument after the Arena. It enjoys a perfect position, standing in front of a wide square whose modest architecture makes the church itself stand out. The subtle and measured design of the pillars, pilaster strips and archwork, the row of mullioned windows and the huge circular window give the whole facade an admirable harmony, to which the ageing of the stone has added a warm golden patina. Under the porch are the portal, done by Maestro Nicolò (about 1138), and the bronze panels of the door which also date back to the 12th century. Of great interest is the Romanesque bell-tower, built in the first half of the 12th century.

House of Juliet. - To the world Verona is not only the city of the Arena and of Cangrande della Scala, but also the city of Romeo and Juliet. This is obvious from the enormous number of tourists who come every year to see the House of Juliet with its famous balcony.

Juliet's Tomb. - In the half-light of a crypt under the Chapel of St. Francis in the former Capuchin friary stands the empty tomb held by long tradition to be that of Shakespeare's heroine. The story, indeed the very existence of Romeo and Juliet, has been questioned by scholars. And yet, even if only a popular legend, the poetic beauty of their love story is so great as almost to convince us that it really happened.

House of Romeo. - In the picturesque Via delle Arche Scaligere, a few steps from the tombs of the rulers of Verona, is this fine 14th century house, said to be the home of the Montague family.

The Arena. - Erected at the beginning of the 1st century A. D., it has reached us in a good state of repair thanks to the « Guardians of the Arena », who had charge of it from 1580 on, and not only rebuilt or shored up crumbling sections but prevented its being defaced by unimaginative attempts at restoration.

PIEVE DI CADORE. - A view of the pleasant valley in which this splendid resort is situated. Behind the blue of the artificial lake and the green of the woods is the magnificent background of the Dolomite peak of Mount Tudaio (nearly 6400 ft.).

LAKE MISURINA. - At an altitude of some 5300 ft. this celebrated Alpine lake has been one of the Cadore region's major attractions for more than 50 years. Like many other parts of the area, it was the scene of fighting during the First World War, when the big hotels it had previously boasted, such as the Grand and the Misurina, were razed to the ground.

CORTINA D'AMPEZZO.
Lying in a magnificent valley through which the Boite flows, surrounded by the highest peaks of the Dolomites (Sorapis, the Tofana peaks, Pomagagnòn, Cristallo, the five « Towers », the « Beak of Midday » and the Lake crag), Cortina d'Ampezzo is Italy's most famous Alpine health resort. Worth noting, at the centre of the photo, is the Ice Stadium built in 1956 for the 7th Winter Olympics. In the background, the magnificent peak of Pomagagnòn.

THREE PEAKS OF LAVAREDO. - The Lavaredo group (over 9000 ft. high), perhaps the most famous of the entire Dolomite range, soars majestically out of the green of the Alpine valley below. In this picture, typical of the Alpine panorama, the warm and varied colour tones highlight nature's solitary beauty.

LAVAREDO: West Peak (9000 ft.) and Great Peak (9100 ft.). - These renowned Dolomite peaks express all the fascination of the mountain. Tall columns of stone, of many different colours in ever-changing combination, they have been the scene of such daring exploits in the relentless struggle between man and rock that they are now part of the Alpine legend.

TRIESTE

A city surrounded by mountains on one side and the sea on the other, Trieste — the ancient Roman city of Tergeste — stands on a gulf in the northernmost part of the Adriatic Sea, between the Zaule valley and the promontory of Miramare. Standing on the promontory like a vision risen from the sea is the tall white castle, scene of the tragic life and loves of the 19th century Austrian prince, Maximilian of Hapsburg. Trieste's whole life is centred on its port, where the lighthouse guides ships into the safety of its harbour. Here you find a city of ample dimensions, as names such as the Grand Canal and the Piazza Grande suggest. From the battlements of the tall medieval Cucherna Tower, the sailors of Trieste looked out on the sea (the tower's name means « lookout » in the Trieste dialect) — the sea where they contended for their livelihood against Turkish pirates and their great maritime neighbours, the Venetians, the sea which breaks on the cliffs of Trieste, caking them with salt and strewing them with seashells. Evidence of Trieste's ancient trade contacts with the Orient can be seen even in its churches such as San Giusto, San Giovanni and the Assunta, whose rich mosaic decorations are reminiscent of Eastern mosques. Noteworthy in Trieste's history is the surge of new life it received around the year 1000. The Adriatic became the city's lifeline, and remained so until Christopher Columbus set out to discover a new route to the East by sailing west but instead discovered the Americas. Trieste's neo-classical architecture of a later era is reminiscent of Vienna, a natural reflection of the city's long ties with Austria. After 500 years of rule by Austria, Trieste felt stirrings of the urge for freedom in 1848, and revolutionaries met in the Tommaso Café, since renamed « Tommaseo » after a hero of the Risorgimento. Later, Oberdan and Nazario Sauro were executed for their part in the fight for freedom; but they had ensured that Trieste would become part of Italy, even though this did not finally take place until the London Agreement of 1954.

Palazzo del Municipio. - This building was erected in 1870 on what is now the Piazza dell'Unità d'Italia, after reorganisation and demolition in this part of the city had turned the square into a vast open-air terrace beside the sea. The people of Trieste still call the square the « Piazza Grande », and it is here that the animated life of the city can be best observed in the cafés spread out in front of the Town Hall's 19th century façade.

San Giusto. - Dedicated to the city's patron saint, this is the Cathedral of Trieste. Actually, it includes two churches side by side, San Giusto and the Assunta (the latter dedicated to the Assumption of the Virgin Mary), which were combined in the 14th century. The Cathedral, which stands high on a hill, is the city's most important building. The Romanesque façade, partially hidden in the photo by the typical Romanesque bell-tower, has a fine Gothic rose-window in the centre. On the marble column in front of the Cathedral is the city's coat-of-arms.

Miramare Castle. - Built in 1854 and designed by the architect Junker for Archduke Maximilian of Austria, brother of the emperor Franz Josef, the castle stands on the edge of a sheer cliff above the sea. It is surrounded by an enormous park of no less than 55 acres, whose design was closely supervised by Maximilian himself. The castle with its white towers has a strong romantic appeal because of the tragic history of the Hapsburg prince who became King of Mexico and was executed during the revolution.

TRENTINO-ALTO ADIGE

Surrounded by important Alpine massifs, between the Rhaetian Alps and the Dolomites, the amalgamated region of Trentino and Alto Adige is where the Italian and Germanic peoples meet. Its mountainous parts, which include most of the Dolomite peaks, give it an exceptional tourist interest. The Dolomites (the name derives from the French scientist Dolomieu who studied the particular limestone of which they are formed) are mountains of exceptional beauty which were created by the erosion of water falling from a limestone plateau of marine deposits. The name Trent derives from the Latin « Tridentum ». The region has two provinces, Trent and Bolzano. Its first inhabitants were Ligurians, forced west by the pressure of the Gauls, and later joined by other Italic peoples such as the Umbrians and the Etruscans. The Romans conquered the area in 110 B.C. and Romanised it so quickly that by 49 B.C. Trent was part of the province of « Venetia and Histria ». When Roman power declined the Trent region was hit by the barbarian invasions: the Alani, Swabians, Vandals, Burgundians, Heruli and Huns wrought havoc in it, until Theodoric, King of the Ostrogoths, imposed his rule on the region, bringing back peace and tranquillity to its peoples. The Bavarians retained the valleys of the Isarco and the Rienzo, while the Longobards continued to rule the other counties of the duchy of Trent. Later the duchy passed into the hands of the Franks, who established the territory of Trent. This territory assumed growing importance because of its geographical position on the communications route between Italy and Germany. At the time of the division of the Roman Empire, the Trent region became part of the Kingdom of Italy; but it was detached in 952 at the wish of the Emperor Otto I, King of Germany, who appropriated the territory so as to give himself a gateway to the south through the Alps. In this period rule was assumed by the bishops whose power was gradually consolidated until they were called on to rule the two principalities of Trent and Bressanone, set up in 1027 by the Emperor Conrad II. These principalities were feudal dependencies of the Holy Roman Empire, and it was for this reason that they passed officially under the Austrian crown in 1511. A new period of struggle began with the death of the last Spanish-Hapsburg sovereign, which triggered off a war of succession between the Hapsburgs and the King of France. At the end of this war, control was strengthened over the two principalities which made up the Trent region, now federated with the Tyrol. The Austrian empress, Maria Theresa, planned to incorporate these territories once and for all, but only after the brief occupation by Napoleon's armies was this project fully realised. In 1803 the two principalities were formally annexed to the Hapsburg Empire, which created a region traditionally autonomous and Italian in spirit but firmly governed by the Austrian Crown. Nevertheless Italian sentiments were kept alive by various associations which although frequently dissolved by the Austrian authorities were reformed with different names. Only at the end of the 1914-18 World War did the region finally come under Italian rule. The heroism of its people was rekindled once more during the last World War: when the Trent region was annexed by the German Reich in 1943, the immediate response was the formation of numerous partisan bands which fought right up until liberation. As if to put a seal on its hard-won reunification with Italy, the area gave her Alcide De Gasperi, Italy's greatest statesman in the post-war period.

BOLZANO

The visitor to Bolzano may find his first contact with the city somewhat disappointing as he drives through the outskirts of a big industrial centre, its cold modern buildings contrasting with the green Alpine slopes and their white huts. This is the price Bolzano has paid for its rapid industrial development. But once inside the old city it is a different story. Here the tourist's expectations are fully satisfied. The northern-style architecture, the narrow streets with their typical verandah-type balconies, the wrought-iron sign-boards which jut out from the buildings, the typical onion-shaped spires of the bell-towers, all contribute to the pleasant atmosphere of an Alpine town. The sensation the city inspires can be summarized in these contrasting aspects. Bolzano is a city of contrast, where different things converge and at times even clash. Here, as indeed in all the places near the border, two civilizations and two ways of life come together. The history itself of the area and the alternations in its government testify to this. A Roman camp in antiquity, then a Bavarian stronghold, Bolzano was later ruled by the powerful Bishop of Trent until 1531, when it passed into the hands of the Tyrol. After being annexed by Napoleon to the Italian Kingdom for a few years, the city returned to and remained under Austrian rule until the end of the Great War. Even in its art — and Bolzano has an important artistic heritage — the city bears the same composite stamp. The frescoes by the Giottesque school of Romagna in the Dominican church contrast with the Gothic cathedral and its multicoloured roof; the typically Tuscan flavour in the construction of the ancient Dominican church stands out against the art of the many 15th and 16th century masters from the Adige region, whose inspiration was clearly northern. Thus in all sides of life in Bolzano, aspects of completely different origin come face to face, each feeling the influence of the other, and form an unusual synthesis.

It is a unique city, which includes contrasts but also affinities, so that the differences which still exist today as in the past can be combined in harmonious coexistence.

SASSOLUNGO GROUP. - A view of the Sassolungo peaks from the Sella Pass: three imposing masses which soar above the green floor of the valley. The group includes, from left, the Sasso di Levante, or « Eastern Peak » (about 9500 ft.), Cinque Dita, « Five Fingers » (over 9000 ft.), and Sassolungo, « Tall Peak », (about 9500 ft.). The peaks have always attracted climbers and are crossed by a network of paths leading up the rock-faces.

TRENT

For Italians, Trent recalls the movement known as « Irredentismo », through which this « unredeemed » territory fought for its freedom from Austrian rule, finally achieved in the First World War. Today the region is more peaceful: in summer its silence is disturbed only by the gurgle of the streams or the songs of the people in its valleys. In Buonconsiglio Castle there are manuscripts containing medieval songs, part of a long tradition of choral music still very much alive, and one hears the sound of water even in the songs: « I went to the fountain this morning. It was so full it overflowed, overflowed in waves. I call my love but she doesn't answer.» Such songs can still be heard in the Tridentine valleys. Trent's name may derive from the ancient « traghetto », or ferry, which crossed the Adige River here where it flows down to Verona. But in the centre of the city, on the square between the cathedral and town hall, is a fountain with a statue of Neptune, the god of the sea, whose striking *tridente* (trident) might seem to have given the city its name. Trent has robust Roman walls, which run up away from the Adige to the Verde tower, then back down to the river. On the mountainsides are houses with wooden terraces decorated with arabesques, where geraniums bloom in the early spring sunshine.

The city is perhaps best known as the site of the Council of Trent, which in the 16th century issued its rulings on Catholic Church doctrine following the upheaval of the Protestant Reformation. But the people of Trent are simple and their customs ancient: they still have the traditional open-air theatre in the square, with characters wearing comic and tragic masks skilfully carved out of tree-bark. At the beginning of spring, the character « Cavra Barbana » makes his appearance; he wears a mask depicting a goat with a beard, as his name signifies, and chases a shepherd wearing a white sheepskin: it represents Spring's victory over Winter. For this festival, the young people of Trent put on their short traditional costumes, dance, and sing their slightly melancholy songs.

Trent. - On the left: Buonconsiglio Castle, whose austere and imposing mass dominates the city. The tower in the centre of the photograph, with its battlemented keep, is the oldest part of the castle. On the right, the facade of the Cathedral, with its huge circular window like an enormous eye. The building was begun in the first half of the 12th century, but not completed until 1515.

MADONNA DI CAMPIGLIO. - Here, in 1188, a refuge was built for pilgrims passing along the road which linked, then as now, the Noce basin and the Lake Garda and Po River regions, crossing the pass of Campo Carlo Magno. Over the centuries a town grew up around the refuge, and in recent years it has grown to considerable importance as an Alpine resort. Madonna di Campiglio, set in a pleasant valley surrounded by woods and dominated by the majestic peaks of the Brenta Dolomites (about 9500 ft. high), is a skier's paradise. Indeed, in the centre of the photograph can be seen the long, steep ski-run of the « Tre-3 », one of the most important ski events held in Italy.

LIGURIA

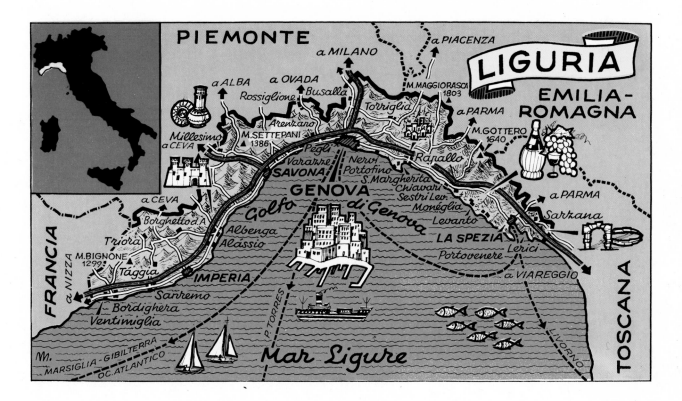

Bounded by the sea, the Maritime Alps and the Ligurian Apennines, Liguria is a hardy, mountainous region, its narrow breadth crossed by short water-courses; but along its shores, among the rugged cliffs, are innumerable gardens and popular seaside resorts. The Ligurians, according to the oldest traditions of the naval art, have always been expert sailors, undaunted by the hardships and perils of the sea. In ancient times the inhabitants of the region pushed northwards, into the Rhone and Po valleys, but in the 6th century B.C., after the Gauls occupied the Po River basin, they were forced to withdraw into the mountainous area near the sea where they were better able to defend themselves. Forced thus to live in this inhospitable territory, their interest turned to the sea, and it was through sea voyages and trading activities that they sought to

gain prosperity. The might of Rome reached out towards the region at an early stage (241 B.C.), but the Romans had to fight for more than a century before overcoming the Ligurians' fierce resistance. After the fall of the Roman Empire, Liguria was invaded by the barbarians; it came under the domination of the Byzantine Empire, then fell into the hands of the Longobards and later the Franks, suffering at the same time from the periodic incursions of the Saracen and Norman raiders. During the feudal era, between the 11th and 12th centuries, the marquisates of Cavi, Lavagna, Savona and Ventimiglia and the counties of Genoa and Nice were founded. Later, however, with the decline of these territories, the powerful bishops gained control of the region, until the rise of the free communes in the city-states, one of the first and most important of which was Genoa. From this point on, the history of Liguria is indissolubly linked to the varying fortunes of Genoa, which gradually subdued the entire region, though it had to contend with difficult problems, including both internal struggles for supremacy among various political factions, and warfare with other states. By 1284, due to its naval victory over the maritime republic of Pisa, which up until then had represented a rival, Genoa had gained unchallenged supremacy in the Mediterranean. Through this supremacy it became rich and powerful, establishing trade ties with cities in both the East and the West. But from 1353 on, the great maritime republic suffered a series of military setbacks at the hands of Venice, and finally came under the control of the Visconti, rulers of Milan, later supplanted by the French. However, in 1538 Andrea Doria, allied with Charles V of Spain, won the battle of Capo d'Orso, thus regaining independence for his native city and ensuring its political and commercial freedom for two centuries. After the French Revolution, Liguria became involved in the various conflicts with the European powers allied against Napoleon, and withstood damaging attacks by the French, English and Austrians, until 1805 when Napoleon became emperor and the region was united to France. After Napoleon's fall, the Congress of Vienna decided to annex Liguria to the Kingdom of Sardinia, and this can be considered the beginning of the energetic activities and resultant gradual change in political climate which contributed so much, in the years between 1849 and 1859, to the formation of a unified Italy. Essential to the work of unification were the political wisdom of Giuseppe Mazzini and military campaigns led by Giuseppe Garibaldi, who embarked with his famous thousand, for the conquest of the Kingdom of the Two Sicilies, from the port of Quarto, near Genoa. After becoming part of the new Italian nation, Liguria was able to resume its maritime activities. The region was unfortunate during the Second World War, suffering grave damages from aerial and naval bombardments; however, 8 September 1943 saw the formation of the Committee for National Liberation, whose partisan forces, as they fought towards eventual victory, saved the region's industrial plants and naval dockyards from destruction by the Germans, thus ensuring that these vital facilities remained intact after the tragic events of the war.

GENOA

A city that is ancient and yet modern. Modern because of the skyscrapers which, seen from the harbour, make it look almost like some transatlantic metropolis. Ancient in the steep, narrow streets which drop dizzyingly down towards the harbour, streets from which the sky seems a ribbon of silk between the red-tiled roofs, so close they almost touch. Ancient in the crowded steps of its brick stairways linking different levels. Modern in the wide curves of the elevated roadway which runs parallel to the sea and gives a splendid view of the port. Ancient in its rituals: from the religious services in the Sanctuary of Madonna della Guardia, to the popular traditions of the « Beating of the Nun » and the « Old Pot ». The former used to take place in Piazza dei Banchi at Mid-Lent, when people ritually beat with a stick the statue of an old woman (perhaps an attack on Lent itself), causing sweetmeats to issue from it. Said to derive from this Genoese tradition is the customary household game of the « Old Pot », now known throughout Italy, in which the blindfolded player tries to break a pot filled with prizes with a stick. Genoa is a genuinely old city around its ancient port, with its tiny old city around its ancient port, with its tiny

shops, fish markets and terrace-like squares cut into the hillsides. An elegant city in the zones up near Brignole Station, and in the higher modern areas where the green of gardens softens the bareness of the sheer cliffs on which the city is built. A seaside city with ancient buildings: the Palazzo Spinola with its famous picture gallery, Palazzo Rosso, Palazzo Bianco, Palazzo Doria, and the Royal Palace whose luminous rooms overlook a park. A modern city with buildings in the Liberty style, all stuccoes, mouldings and coloured terracotta. A city with a theatrical tradition, revived since the War by the « Little Theatre of Genoa » with its avant-garde repertoire. A city of artists like Paganini, tempestuous virtuoso of the violin, and Barabino, who painted in the blue tones of the sea. A city of patriots like Mazzini, or Cesare Abba and Nino Bixio, who set out from nearby with Garibaldi on the expedition to invade Sicily. A city of poets like the Montale of our time, and prose writers like Camillo Sbarbaro of an earlier epoch. But a city whose modern dockyards and latter-day glories do not make her forget her ancient, proud title of « Superba ».

The Cathedral. - Dedicated to St. Lawrence, it was rebuilt and consecrated by Pope Gelasius in 1118, though its origins are older still. Imposing and severe in appearance, it is an admirable combination of many styles which indicate the long period of time taken to complete its construction; in fact, it includes Romanesque, Gothic and Renaissance elements. The graceful facade, dressed in black and white marble, has a fine rose-window in the centre. On the right is the belltower on which Michele Pessolo and Domenico da Caranca worked; it was completed only in 1552. The close links of the cathedral of St. Lawrence with the history of Genoa are shown by the numerous references to the church in early documents.

Palazzo Ducale. - Ancient residence of the Doges of the Republic, it was built in 1291, but of this earliest construction there are only a few remains visible along the left-hand side of the building. Rebuilt in the 16th century by Andrea Vannone, it was enriched by numerous works of art including the frescoes of Aldovrandini and Franceschini, and the paintings of Solimene da Napoli. After the disastrous fire in 1777 which destroyed most of the building, it was restored by public subscription; it was at this time that the neo-classical facade with double columns was added, the work of Simone Cantoni. Shortly afterwards at the time of the popular revolution of 1797, the building was considerably defaced in attempts to wipe out all trace of its aristocratic origins.

SESTRI LEVANTE. - A beautiful haven built along the sea-front like all the villages of the Riviera, especially in this part of it which is known as the Riviera di Levante. Its white houses and little churches with pointed bell-towers stand back to back against sheer cliffs above the sea. And the sea governs the rhythm of the inhabitants' existence, lived out between the town's steep little streets and the beach, where the nets lie drying, ready to be stowed aboard the trawlers once again. The adjacent Gulf of Tigullio is a reminder of the old Roman name for the town, *Segesta Tigulliorum*, of which the first half has been shortened and italianised into Sestri. Immediately inland grow wild pines, prickly pears, lemons and oranges. And there are fertile nurseries for the carnations of the Riviera, which bloom quickly and easily in the mild climate. The carriages of the local train, which runs lazily along the coast, stopping briefly at all stations even when the popular beach resorts are empty, pick up these sweet-smelling flowers and transport them all over the country. They are carried in baskets of cane, deftly woven in soft colours, on which the place they come from is clearly stamped in black letters — as if to draw attention to Sestri Levante's exceptionally sunny climate.

CAMOGLI. - Strung out along the sea, Camogli also depends for its livelihood on the sea. Famous for its « Fish Festival », where visitors are offered fish freshly fried in an enormous pan, its origins go far back in time. Archaeological discoveries make it reasonable to suppose that there was already a village here in the 2nd century A.D. A flourishing commercial centre at the time of the maritime republics, it had trade contacts as far as Majorca. In the 19th century Garibaldi's expedition employed a skilful pilot from Camogli, Salvatore Schiaffino, who knew the sea so perfectly he was able to guide the none too seaworthy vessels all the way to Sicily. For Camogli's inhabitants the sea has always been the only important thing in life, as can be seen by the boats of every shape and size moored in front of the fishermen's homes, the floating dwellings in which they spend half of their lives.

PORTOFINO. - A natural port protected by its promontory, Portofino is one of the most beautiful places on the Ligurian Riviera and has been famous ever since the time of the Romans, when it was mentioned by Pliny. Its many-coloured houses are built around the harbour in the form of a huge amphitheatre — a typical example of the dynamic way in which the restricted amount of building space has been exploited in the towns of the Riviera. The elegant yachts swinging at anchor on the harbour are a reminder of the fact that Portofino is one of Italy's most fashionable summer resorts.

PORTOVENERE. - « Port of Venus »: a name that is like a promise maintained. It is as if beauty itself was born here among the blue stretches of sea, white churches and fishermen's houses, overlooked by the turrets and battlements of a castle. The castle stands near a thick wood whose pines run down to the beach. The blue of the sea, reflecting the sun, gives its walls a reflection like mother-of-pearl. And yet in earlier times war reached even Portovenere, which was fortified in the 13th century by the Genoese against attacks by their enemies, the Pisans, from nearby Lerici. Now the echo of medieval battles between the maritime republics for control of the Mediterranean — and all that this meant — has long since died away. Portovenere today bathes in the splendour of the sea, a sea beautiful even when it is stormy, breaking high on the cliffs and almost threatening the little houses nearby. It is a much frequented swimming resort, but one without fashionable pretensions.

EMILIA AND ROMAGNA

Industry and widespread agricultural development have made this region one of the
richest in Italy. Its plain, lying between the
Ligurian Apennines and those of Tuscany
and Emilia, drains into the Adriatic Sea,
and thriving cities lie along its imaginary
backbone, the old Roman road called the

Via Aemilia. Its people are courteous, jovial
and open-hearted, and they have stored up
an immense artistic and cultural heritage,
much of it owed to the genius of artists
born in the region itself. Back in the Paleo-
lithic and Neolithic Ages, it seems that its
first inhabitants were of Iberian and Ligur-

ian stock; in the Bronze Age, peoples of Italic origin conquered the region, and in the Iron Age there was the Villanovian civilisation, followed by the Etruscans (7th century B.C.). The Etruscans gave way to the Gauls, but these too fell before the advance of the Romans who succeeded in occupying the entire region between 201 and 191 B.C. Under Roman domination, the region assumed its present name, derived from the Roman road known as the Via Aemilia, which links Rimini and Piacenza and was built in 187 B.C. under the consul Marcus Aemilius Lepidus. With the division of the Roman Empire into East and West, the city of Ravenna became the capital of the territory controlled by the Eastern Byzantine Empire in the West, but after a long period of Byzantine domination it was easy prey for the invading barbarians. In 568 it was conquered by the Longobards, and was virtually divided into two parts: the territory of the Exarchate, which took its name from the « exarchs », the Byzantine governors, included the cities of Ravenna, Bologna, Ferrara, Adria and other smaller settlements, and remained under the gradually diminishing rule of the Byzantine Empire; and the Pentapolis, which united the cities of Ancona, Pesaro, Fano, Umana and Osino. Because of the strong preponderance of Romans there, the first of these two parts came to be called Romania, whence the present-day name of Romagna. During the Longobard rule, their leaders tried several times to conquer the territory of the Exarchate, and finally succeeded in doing so in 751. However, this conquest prompted a reaction by the Papacy, which felt its territory menaced and appealed for aid to the Franks. The latter, having defeated the Longobards, divided the territory into numerous duchies, and presented the Exarchate to the Pope — although papal control of the area was to become effective only in the 13th century. The period which followed saw the birth of the free communes in reaction to oppression by the wealthy feudal lords. But, as happened in so many other parts of Italy, the ambitions of various rich and powerful families led to the formation of *signorie*, single families ruling over various cities: thus between the 13th and 15th centuries we find the Da Polenta family in Ravenna, the Pepoli and Bentivoglio in Bologna, the Malatesta in Rimini, the Odelaffi in Forlì, the Estensi in Ferrara, the Visconti in Piacenza. Political, economic and religious interests caused various changes of government in Emilia and Romagna, according to the fortune at arms of the different contenders; but the Papacy managed to prevail little by little and to impose its authority on almost the whole region. In the middle of the 18th century the region was subdivided into the Duchy of Parma and Piacenza and the Duchy of Modena and Reggio, with the rest (Romagna plus part of Emilia) as part of the Papal States. This situation was to continue virtually until the unification of Italy, except for the brief Napoleonic period during which the region was part of the Italian Kingdom. During the Italian Risorgimento, the Emilians strongly supported liberation, organising conspiracies, movements such as the Carbonari secret societies, and revolts in the cities. And from this region came Italy's present-day national flag, the tricolour, which was devised at Reggio by representatives of Emilian cities on the occasion of the proclamation of the Cispadane Republic in 1797. During the last World War too, the courageous spirit of the Emilian people came clearly to the forefront. When the Allied armies were brought to a halt on the Apennines in the autumn of 1944 by the existence of the Gothic Line, they formed vigorous partisan groups which actually managed to liberate small areas of territory, and keep them independent. The Emilians paid a heavy price for joining in the fighting, and among the many one name above all symbolises their heroism: Marzabotto, where practically the whole population was exterminated as a reprisal by German troops.

BOLOGNA

Among Italians there are two phrases applied to Bologna: *Bologna la dotta* (« the learned ») and *Bologna la grassa* (« the fat »).

The first refers to its famous university — the first in Europe and one of the largest in medieval times — which in the 19th century had a renewal of fame from the presence of two great poets, Pascoli and Carducci, and the scholar Zanichelli who founded a flourishing publishing house.

The second refers to the inhabitants' love of good cheer. The Bolognese love to eat well, washing down with their sparkling Lambrusco wine the tasty local specialities like *zampone, cotechino* and the pasta dish *tortello*. This last is the favourite dish of Doctor Balanzone, the fat Bolognese doctor whose name in Italian suggests both learning and hearty eating, a stock character of the old popular comedy. He typifies the Bolognese temperament, easily won over by friendship, and fond of a pleasant siesta.

The city itself is similar: the colour of its bricks gives its unique architecture an immediately friendly, communicative quality. Its arcades with their rounded archways shelter the footpaths in every street from the rain and the snow which falls frequently in Emilia, the region surrounding Bologna. One escapes from the humid atmosphere of the grey, bare plain into the quiet and shade of the corridor-like arcades, which resemble in a way the canals lined with rows of poplars running through the fields in this part of Emilia. Water in the country, and shelter from water in the city.

Up on the hill is the soft green setting of the church of San Michele in Bosco, said to have been built after a dove had outlined its plan on the ground with golden straws.

Going higher still, one can walk two miles up the hillside through the long corridor of arcades, looking as though they were red-coloured pipes of a fantastic organ, to reach the Sanctuary which contains a portrait of Our Lady supposed to have been painted by St. Luke the Evangelist.

Bologna from up here is a veritable forest of domes and bell-towers, threaded together by winding arcades of that unmistakable colour which resembles vine-leaves in autumn. Highest of all stand the two towers of Garisenda and Asinelli, which are the symbol of the city and a reminder of the liberties and rights established long ago in the free Commune of Bologna.

Piazza del Nettuno - Jean Boulogne, called Giambologna (1529-1608): *Fountain of Neptune.*

Palace of King Enzo. - It takes its name from its most famous guest, even if his stay was compulsory and his palace a gilded prison. Enzo, son of Frederick II of Sicily and Bianca Lancia, received the title of King of Sardinia when he married Adelasia of Gallura. Captured by the Bolognese at the battle of Fossalta in 1249 while fighting by his father's side against the Guelf communes, he remained a prisoner until his death in 1279. Brought up at his father's court where the poets Jacopo da Lantini and Pier della Vigna wrote, he had poetic ambitions himself which he pursued during his long imprisonment.

Palazzo del Podestà. - Standing beside the Palace of King Enzo, it looks out on the wide square of Piazza Maggiore. It was built in its present form between 1484 and 1494, designed by Aristotele Fioravanti. The building is dominated by the solid, square tower of the Arrengo, which was part of an earlier 13th-century structure.

San Petronio. - This massive church dominates the Piazza Maggiore. Built to a design by Antonio di Vincenzo, with three naves in the Gothic style, the lower section of its marble-covered facade frames the fine portal by Jacopo della Quercia, a masterpiece of this artist. Over this doorway in 1508 was placed Michelangelo's bronze statue of Pope Julius II. Unfortunately in 1511, during a popular tumult caused by a brief return to power of the Bentivoglio family, the statue of the unpopular pope was pulled down and destroyed completely.

Garisenda and Asinelli Towers. - These can be considered the emblem of the city of Bologna, a testimony of its resistance to domination and its independence during the Middle Ages. Standing very close to each other, the towers are visible from every part of the city. The taller of the two (about 300 ft. high) was built between 1109 and 1119 by the Asinelli family, whereas the other belonged to the Garisenda family; it was previously much higher but it had to be lowered in 1360, because it had begun to lean dangerously (its present divergence from the vertical is about 10 ft.). The towers, built for defence purposes, could be rapidly transformed into impregnable fortresses, while long beams could be extended from the narrow windows making it possible to pass from one besieged building to the other.

PIACENZA

Palazzo Comunale. - A splendid example of the Lombard Gothic style of architecture, this building was constructed towards the end of the 13th century. Among the builders were Pietro da Cagnano, Gherardo Campanaro, Negro Negri and Pietro da Borghetto. The massive open portico in white stone, with a light tinge of pink, is lightened by its Gothic arches. The portico and the brick section above, with its delicate three-mullioned windows, make this one of the finest buildings of its type in Italy.

The Cathedral. - Begun in 1122, Piacenza's cathedral was completed in 1233 by the architect Rainaldo da Sambuceto and is one of the most outstanding works of Romanesque architecture in the Emilia region. The facade, with its splendid rose-window, has a sober beauty. On the left of the Cathedral stands the massive brick bell-tower, built in 1333, and on the top of its spire is an angel, sculpted in wood and coated with gilded copper, by Mastro Vago. Hanging suspended in space just below the bell-chamber can be seen an iron cage: Ludovico Sforza, called Ludovico il Moro, had the cage placed here in 1495, as a form of punishment for persons convicted of sacrilege.

FERRARA

Estense Castle. - This imposing masterpiece of military architecture from the late Middle Ages (it was completed in 1385) was built for Nicolò II d'Este, one of the most prominent members of the Estense family, which by that time had established uncontested rule over Ferrara. Designed by Bartolino Plotino, the massive brick castle is mirrored in the wide moat surrounding it. The battlements which originally ran round the top of its walls were removed during restoration work in the 16th century.

The Cathedral. - The outstanding marble facade, in which Romanesque and Gothic motifs are combined in unusual harmony, makes this an extremely picturesque building. The cathedral, dedicated to St. George, was designed by Nicolò, a pupil of the great Wiligelmo, on a commission from Guglielmo degli Adelardi. It was built in 1135. The lower, Romanesque part of the facade includes the three portals; particularly noteworthy is the central portal with its porch resting on columns supported by statues of lions and caryatids (female figures of classical derivation). The loggia above and its magnificent « Last Judgment », a masterpiece of 13th century sculpture, represents a turning point in the art of the Emilian region. The bell-tower on the right of the cathedral was built in 1412 to a design by Leon Battista Alberti, and is the first example of Renaissance architecture at Ferrara.

RAVENNA

Ravenna stands out among the cities of Emilia and Romagna because of its unique character, which gives it a fascination unimpaired by time. Once known as « Ravenna the silent », it has been transformed in the period since the war into an increasingly important industrial centre. The history of the city is closely linked to the development of Western civilization. From here Caesar set out with his legions to conquer Rome, and here Augustus established one of his bases for the Roman fleet. First under Odoacer and later under Theodoric it became capital of the states established after the fall of the Roman Empire. Under the dominion of the Byzantines it was the last bulwark of the Western half of the divided Empire. A number of superb buildings still remain today to testify to Ravenna's importance in these periods. Besides its civic buildings, among which the most imposing is the Palace of Theodoric, there are the basilicas of Sant'Apollinare in Classe, San Vitale, Sant'Apollinare Nuovo and San Giovanni Evangelista, as well as the two baptistries, all built through the tireless activities of Ravenna's earliest archbishops. The city, whose canal-port of Corsini is on the Adriatic Sea, is also renowned for its mausoleums: the tombs of Galla Placidia and of Theodoric. But above all Ravenna is famous for its mosaics. As one writer has put it: « An understanding of colour never since equalled permitted these artists to use the most beautiful of tones to cover the insides of the apses, the ceilings of the domes, the sides of the naves, and the triumphal arches of their churches ». A reminder of Venetian influence is the tomb of Dante, who completed his poetic masterpiece, the « Divine Comedy », and ended his days in Ravenna. The Venetian governor Bernardo Bembo commissioned Pietro Lombardo to create the marble bust of the great poet which adorns his tomb. At Ravenna is the pine-forest celebrated by Dante and Byron, where Anita Garibaldi, wife of the hero of Italian unification, died when they were escaping together from Rome.

Ravenna. - Sant'Apollinare in Classe.

Sant'Apollinare in Classe. - When Ravenna was chosen as the base for the Roman Empire's Adriatic fleet during the reign of the emperor Augustus, the construction of a new port became necessary. A site was chosen a little south of the city, and here the port of Classe was created: the name derives from the Latin « Classis Praetoria », meaning « fleet of the Emperor ». Around it a town of considerable size quickly grew up. In this town during the 6th century this magnificent basilica was built, commissioned by Bishop Ursicinus and financed by the munificence of Julianus Argentarius. It was dedicated to the memory of Bishop Apollinaris, who had converted the region to Christianity and died a martyr, and consecrated in the year 549 by Archbishop Maximinian. The magnificent interior consists of three naves divided by 24 huge columns of grained marble, crowned by Byzantine capitals with their characteristic perforated leaf design. The altar in the middle of the nave is the original one used in the consecration of the church.

Battistero Neoniano. - Also called the « Battistero degli Ortodossi » (Baptistry of the Orthodox), this is Ravenna's oldest building; it stands beside the Cathedral. Thought to have originally been a public bath-house (as its plan clearly suggests), the building was converted into a church by Bishop Orsus at the beginning of the 5th century. It is octagonal in plan. Inside there are eight columns supporting upper walls decorated with stuccos which were formerly gilded. On the inside of the dome is a series of mosaics which according to documentary evidence were commissioned by Bishop Neo between 449 and 452. The baptistry's present name derives from this bishop.

San Vitale. - The builder of the original basilica, one of the purest examples of Byzantine architecture in Italy, is unknown. But the construction was financed by Julianus Argentarius, at a cost of no less than 26,000 gold pieces.

San Vitale. Interior. - The interior, octagonal in plan, is of exceptional beauty, due both to its unique design and to the wealth of its marble work. The superb arches, capitals, stuccos, and mosaics create a harmony rivalled only by the singular effect of the galleries, built one on top of the other around the walls of the church.

San Vitale. Interior of the Apse. - *Mosaic.* On the circular wall of the apse is this splendid Byzantine mosaic depicting Christ, with two angels by his side, in the act of offering the triumphal crown to St. Vitalis. On the other side, Bishop Ecclesius, who was responsible for the building of the church, presents a model of it.

San Vitale. Interior. - *Mosaic of the Presbytery.* - The series of mosaics in the presbytery of San Vitale are believed to have been inspired by a Romanesque school. The figures depicted are less static than those of the preceding Byzantine tradition, and at times the forms of the body itself are suggested under the clothing. On the page at right are the mosaics which depict, above, the emperor Justinian preceded by clergy and followed by officials and soldiers; below, the empress Theodora with her train of two ministers and seven matrons.

MAXIMIANVS

Mausoleum of Galla Placidia. - Standing not far from San Vitale, this monument was built by Galla Placidia, mother of the emperor Valentinian III. According to a not very reliable tradition, her remains were brought here for burial when she died in 450; a sarcophagus inside the building is still pointed out to visitors as the one which contained her body. The building is simple but effective in design and contains a series of mosaics of considerable beauty.

Mausoleum of Galla Placidia. Interior. - *The Good Shepherd.*

Mausoleum of Galla Placidia. Interior. - In the niches under the vaults, with their superbly imaginative series of mosaics, are a number of sarcophagi. The tombs were transferred here in the 14th century; the one at the centre of the photo is traditionally held to be that of Galla Placidia. In the lunette is a mosaic depicting St. Lawrence on his way to be roasted alive.

Sant'Apollinare Nuovo. - Built by Theodoric, probably between 495 and 525 (during the period when the Goths ruled Ravenna), this was originally a church of the Arian cult. But it was later handed over by the Arians to the Catholic Church following an edict issued by the emperor Justinian, and in about 560 Bishop Agnellus reconsecrated the basilica, dedicating it to St. Martin, an implacable opponent of the Arian heresy. Its present name derives from the fact that in the 9th century the remains of Bishop Apollinaris were brought here from the church of Sant'Apollinare in Classe.

Sant'Apollinare Nuovo. Interior. *Mosaics on the right-hand wall.* This wall is divided horizontally into three series of mosaic decorations. The top series depicts scenes from the life of Christ, the middle series figures of the saints, Church fathers and prophets, and the lower series a view of the city of Ravenna showing the facade of the Palace of Theodoric, together with a procession of virgins with crowns in their hands.

Sant'Apollinare Nuovo. Interior. - A magnificent series of 24 columns of Greek marble with Corinthian capitals divides the interior of Sant'Apollinare Nuovo into three naves, creating an orderly, solemn distribution of space. The columns stand out dramatically because of the cushion-shaped support on the top of each capital, separating it from the arch above, and thus isolating the column itself. The apse at the end of the church is a recent acquisition: it was reconstructed in 1950 after the remains of the original structure had been uncovered by excavation. This is another of Ravenna's churches whose huge walls and ceilings are covered with magnificent mosaics. These may be divided into two sections according to their different styles: the upper part, including scenes from the life of Christ and figures of the saints, which is in the Hellenistic-Roman style and dates from the beginning of the 6th century; and the lower part, in the Byzantine style, dating from about the second half of the 6th century. In the 16th century the floor of the church was raised about 4 feet, and to avoid sacrificing part of the columns the arches were raised and the walls cut away. This destroyed stucco decorations which are mentioned in the « Liber Pontificalis », by the 9th-century historian Andrea Agnello. It is worth remarking that around the church's portico there were previously mosaics which depicted figures apparently linked to its period as a church of the Arian cult; they were obliterated when it was handed over to the Catholic faith. Of these figures, some hands remain, and above the level of the drapes there are outlines of heads left when the mosaic was detached.

RIMINI

« The land where the traveller is greeted by the azure beauty of San Marino ». The aptness of these famous verses, freely translated from Pascoli's poem, « Romagna », becomes clear to the traveller when he nears Rimini, and as he travels through this part of Romagna he is always aware of the tiny, enchanting republic of San Marino in the distance. From Rimini itself the dominating feature of the countryside is the peak of Monte Titano on which San Marino stands, so much a part of the city that the visitor comes to look for it as his most familiar point of reference. Rimini, the natural centre of the splendid Adriatic Riviera, is one of the best-known of the seaside resorts which have expanded so enormously through tourism in recent years: in fact, its normal population of 100,000 grows to five times that number during the summer months. But while most seaside resorts, large or small, in any country, are simply building developments strung out along the sea-front to serve the holiday-makers, Rimini is different. It has preserved its identity, and remained a city in its own right. Indeed, it is a historic and artistic centre of first importance, with a great heritage of traditions, historic buildings and works of art — besides being an industrious modern city. Rimini has the advantage of being situated in a beautiful and fertile region, whose abundant harvests include fruit and wines. Its people are pleasant and open-hearted, and its cuisine is justly famous.

Bridge of Tiberius. - An important Roman construction which surprisingly has reached us almost completely intact: only the final arch, which was destroyed by the Goths in 580, has since been reconstructed. Spanning the Marecchia River, it was begun under the emperor Augustus in 14 A.D. and completed by Tiberius in 21 A.D.

Palazzo dell'Arengo. - Symbolising the greatness of the free Commune of Rimini during the Middle Ages, the Palazzo dell'Arengo, constructed between 1204 and 1207, is the city's major civic building.

Arch of Augustus. - Built in 27 B.C., this is the most ancient of all the surviving Roman arches. It was erected as a tribute to Caesar Augustus. The arch has always been part of the city walls, and has therefore been considerably altered and adapted to the needs of different ages.

Tempio Malatestiano. - This church is not only the most important and famous of Rimini's buildings, but also one of the most interesting examples of Italian Renaissance architecture. It has been called « contradictory », because its interior and exterior are completely different in design and conception; and yet perhaps this very contradiction partly explains its perpetual fascination. It dates back to the rule of Sigismondo Pandolfo Malatesta, who had already had two chapels built inside the church of San Francesco, when in 1450, at the height of his power, he commissioned a completely new design for the church's exterior by the Florentine architect Leon Battista Alberti. Alberti designed a classical exterior which be saw simply as a noble «prelude » to his central plan: a huge apse surmounted by an equally magnificent cupola. Unfortunately work was suspended when Malatesta died; and the structure conceived by Alberti was never fully realised.

Tempio Malatestiano. Interior. - When Malatesta commissioned Alberti for the church's exterior, he entrusted the interior to the Veronese Matteo de' Pasti. Pasti's design was undisguisedly Gothic in style, despite the classical lines of the pillars, pilaster strips and festoons. This division of the designers' tasks and the completely different conceptions of the two artists led to the intriguing « contradictions » to be seen in the building.

SAN MARINO

San Marino is a symbol of independence and freedom. This tiny republic, with a population of 15,000 and an area of less than 24 square miles, is said to be the smallest in the world. Legend has it that it was founded in 301 by the stonemason Marino, who came from Dalmatia and established the republic here, relying on the rugged mountainside to defend its villages and castles. The republic proudly maintained its independence against kings and popes, princes and soldiers of fortune, resisting military attacks and political manoeuvres alike. Among the innumerable states of all shapes and sizes — principalities, oligarchies and communes — into which Italy was divided after the fall of the Roman Empire, San Marino is the only one which has kept its independence intact. The republic has maintained its ancient political system, though it has been brought up to date as changing times have demanded. Thus its basic governing bodies are still known by the names familiar in so many medieval Italian city-states: the « Arengo », the « Consiglio Grande e Generale », the « Congresso di Stato », the « Congresso dei Dodici », and finally the « Capitani Reggenti », the political leaders with executive power. The « Capitani Reggenti » are elected twice a year, in March and September, and their election is followed by picturesque installation ceremonies on April 1 and October 1. San Marino has its own flag, with blue and white horizontal stripes, and its own military Corps (the « Guardia di Rocca » and « Guardia di Consiglio », the « Milizia » and « Gendarmeria »). It also maintains diplomatic relations with the most important countries. Visitors from all parts of the world — attracted by its history, its unique situation, the hospitality of its inhabitants, its tasty cuisine and the original products of its artisans — fill the streets, squares and castles of this unusual place all the year round.

Palazzo Pubblico. - The most important of San Marino's civic buildings, it has the typical appearance of a fortress, with its square base, high walls and towers, rows of Gothic arches on the ground floor and tall Gothic windows above them. Originally the *Domus magna communis*, the seat of the city's governing body built at the end of the 14th century, stood on this site. It was reconstructed several times, and the building in its present form was erected between 1884 and 1894 on a design by the architect Francesco Azzurri. In the centre of the square is S. Galletti's statue of « Liberty », created in 1896. The statue was presented to the city by an Englishwoman, Othillia Heyoth Galletti, who was rewarded for her gesture by receiving the title of Duchess of Acquaviva.

Porta San Francesco. - This is the most interesting of the many gates in the walls of San Marino. Also called « Porta del Locho », it is set in a Gothic archway under a square, battlemented tower which is part of the third circle of city walls. Under the archway can still be seen two inscriptions which state laws of transit prescribed by the statutes of San Marino in the 17th century.

TUSCANY

The very individual character of the region of Tuscany is something which is unmistakeable and which exists despite its many local peculiarities. The region is clearly defined to the north by the Apennine mountains between Tuscany and Emilia, though in the upper part of the Tiber Valley and further to the south its characteristics, mainly of a linguistic and historical nature, are less definite. Tuscany is shaped roughly like a heart and lies in the centre of the Italian peninsula, with its sunny islands, including Elba, off the coast to the west.

The name of Tuscany is linked to the most important events in the history of Italy, from the time when the Etruscans (from whom its name derives) conquered the region and made it the centre of their magnificent civilisation, fascinating evidence of which remains in the cities of Cerveteri, Vulci, Roselle, Volterra, Arezzo, Populonia, Chiusi, Vetulonia and Fiesole. In their period of maximum expansion, the Etruscans extended their territory north to the Po River and south, through Latium and Rome, to Campania. Later, however, this people, which had emigrated here from the Middle East, was pushed back by pressure from the Gauls and the Romans into present-day Tuscany, which became at the time of Augustus the seventh region of the Italian peninsula. The barbarian invasions did not pass Tuscany by, and it was ruled for a time by the Longobard dukes. In the Dark Ages, control and defence of the region was in the hands of the count-bishops, and the first feudal strongholds were established.

However, a new spirit of liberty was born in the 12th century with the beginning of the struggles between the city-dwellers and the feudal barons based in the country. The turmoil of the new era made possible the burgeoning development of the cities, which profited from the conflict between Church and Empire to win their independence.

In Tuscany, and especially in Florence, new forms of expression came into being, above all the language of the region which, derived from low Latin, was to become the language of the whole of Italy. And it was in Tuscany that the first forms of modern democratic government were born: in the republics, which maintained citizens' rights despite violent internal struggles; the illuminated autocratic rule of the first Medici, including Cosimo the Elder and Lorenzo the Magnificent; and the later battles fought in the name of liberty at Florence and Monte San Savino.

The conquest by the Medici grand dukes of Pisa, Arezzo, Cortona and Siena, plus their peace treaties with Lucca and Genoa, ushered in an era of unprecedented economic prosperity for Tuscany — a prosperity so great that the bankers of Florence and Lucca were able to lend millions of gold florins (the coin originally minted in Florence) to the King of England himself. In the era of the Medici grand dukes, Florence conquered many other cities, such as Pisa, Arezzo and Cortona, and concluded peace treaties with others, such as Lucca and Genoa. Nor did the splendid culture of Tuscany come to an end when the Medici dynasty died out: the Lorraine family, under whose rule the region came in 1748, maintained the high standards of their predecessors. During the era of the Risorgimento, Tuscany became a refuge for those free spirits who dreamed of independence from Austria and the formation of a unified Italian nation. After a bloodless revolution which lasted a single day, a plebiscite was held on 15 March 1860 and Tuscany elected to become part of the new Kingdom of Italy.

The history of Tuscany has thus been in many ways a process of logical development, at whose centre has always been the concept of the freedom of man. Each city in the region has a long and glorious artistic tradition with clearly defined individual characteristics, though their mutual inspiration can also be discerned. Renaissance Florence is very different from Gothic Siena, Pisa's Romanesque style different again from that of Lucca, and the Etruscan city of Volterra has features distinguishing it from Arezzo.

FLORENCE

« Standing on the hill of San Miniato and looking down, as so many have done, at the city spread out at our feet, we see before us a city such as none other can be, one in which things have had their birth which now form the life-blood of the intellectual existence of Europe. Her outward beauty is palpable to all ». This is the beginning of *The Medici*, G. F. Young's history of Florence's most famous family. Florence's beauty is indeed obvious to any visitor. It derives not simply from the splendid individual monuments, but from the harmonious whole created by its churches and civic buildings, the narrow and picturesque streets of the historic centre, and the city's perfect natural setting. To understand Florence, however, one needs to grasp something more, something which might be called the city's peculiar genius. Evidence of this genius can be seen in the monuments created in every epoch of its long and brilliant history — such as the Baptistry built in the 11th century (though part of it probably goes back to the 5th century), the Palazzo Vecchio and the Piazzale Michelangelo overlooking the city, created last century. The city seems to have had two important centres during its early history: that of the Roman military encampment, whose regular outlines are reflected in the layout of the streets around Piazza della Repubblica (although almost nothing has remained of Roman Florence); and the Medieval and Renaissance centre around Piazza della Signoria, closer to the River Arno. From here bridges were built, first the Ponte Vecchio and later others, which the Florentines crossed to extend their dominion over the surrounding area. The focal point of Florence's history was the Palazzo Vecchio, standing on Piazza Signoria with its famous statues, including the symbolic lion called the « Marzocco » by Donatello, Cellini's « Perseus » and Michelangelo's « David ». The events in the Palazzo Vecchio, the city's centre of government, lie behind Florence's emergence from the Middle Ages, and progress through Humanism to the Renaissance. In this period, from the 13th to the 16th century, Florence was the centre of European culture. This was also the period when its greatest works of art were realised, first under democratic rule and later under the enlightened autocracy of the Medici. Again when Florence became capital of the newly formed Kingdom of Italy last century, there was a regeneration out of which came works of art already recognised as classics of their kind.

The Baptistry. - Dante, who was baptised here, referred to it as *il bel San Giovanni*. In the Romanesque style, it was built between the 11th and 12th centuries. Octagonal in plan, it is surrounded on the outside by a double order of pillars which support a series of arches; the exterior is dressed in marble, and divided into orderly sections by the juxtaposition of the white stone of Carrara and the green stone of Prato. Dedicated to San Giovanni Battista - St. John the Baptist - it was Florence's cathedral until 1128.

Porta del Paradiso. - These are the eastern doors of the Baptistry and derive their name from the fact that Michelangelo was so impressed by their beauty he pronounced them fit to be the gates of Paradise. The gilt bronze doors are the crowning achievement of Lorenzo Ghiberti who devoted no less than 27 years to the work (from 1425 to 1452), calling on his profound knowledge of the moulder's art to create a richly imaginative and flawlessly composed masterpiece. He must certainly have satisfied the Merchants' Guild which commissioned him for the work, stipulating that he « create it in whatever manner he pleased, but that he seek to the best of his ability to make it as ornate, rich, perfect and beautiful as could be imagined; nor should time or expense be spared to create a masterpiece transcending all his other works. » Michelozzo, Benozzo Gozzoli and Bernardo Cennini collaborated with Ghiberti in creating the doors, which have 10 panels depicting scenes from the Bible.

Santa Maria del Fiore. - Florence's majestic Cathedral was begun in 1296 by Arnolfo di Cambio, who had been charged by the Republic with creating a work « as lofty and magnificent as the genius and ability of man can achieve. » It was built on the site of a former Cathedral, Santa Reparata, opposite the Baptistry of San Giovanni. When Arnolfo died in 1302, work was interrupted; it was resumed in 1334 under the direction of Giotto, who had previously been responsible for constructing the bell-tower. On Giotto's death in 1337, the project lost momentum; then between 1357 and 1364 the committee directing the work appointed Lapo Ghini and Francesco Talenti, and commissioned them to prepare a plan even more grandiose in its proportions than that of Arnolfo. Finally in 1366 the definitive plan was presented by four architects; work proceeded at a much faster pace and in 1378 the vault above the central nave was completed. In 1418, tenders were called for the construction of the cupola; the project was awarded to Filippo Brunelleschi, even though he refused to exhibit his model for fear of having it copied. Brunelleschi completed this architectural and engineering masterpiece between 1420 and 1434, and in 1436 Pope Eugene IV consecrated the Cathedral, solemnly dedicating it to Our Lady with the title of Santa Maria del Fiore.

The Cathedral. Facade. - The facade, which had been left uncompleted up until the 19th century, was designed by the architect Emilio de Fabris. De Fabris, who began work in 1871, took his inspiration from the Florentine Gothic style. The statues he added were done by contemporary sculptors.

Bell-tower by Giotto. - The 250ft. high bell-tower of the Cathedral, built more than 500 years ago, remains today one of the most beautiful structures of its kind in the world. Commissioned to build it by the governing body of Florence, Giotto completed his model of the tower in 1334, and the foundations of the huge structure were laid in July of the same year. Unfortunately three years later Giotto died, and work was continued by Andrea Pisano until 1359, and completed by Francesco Talenti. Both adhered scrupulously to the design of their great predecessor, with the sole exception of the spire which was to have added 30ft. to the top of the tower, but which was never constructed.

Santa Maria del Fiore. Interior. - MICHELANGELO BUONARROTI (1475-1564): *Pietà.* This dramatic marble sculpture was begun by the artist at the age of seventy-five, and was intended to be placed on his tomb. However, it remained uncompleted at his death.

Loggia della Signoria. - Built by Benci di Cione and Simone di Francesco Talenti between 1376 and 138?, it was once known as the « Loggia dell'Orcagna » because of the traditional belief that it had been designed by the great artist Orcagna, who died in 1368; it was also called the « Loggia dei Lanzi » because at the time of the Medici ruler Cosimo I it served as quarters for the Landsknechten, his German mercenary soldiers. Originally it was used by Florence's rulers for civil and religious ceremonies. Covered by graceful cruciform vaults, it contains numerous famous works of sculpture from various epochs.

Loggia della Signoria. - BENVENUTO CELLINI (1500-1571): *Perseus.*

Piazza della Signoria. - Surrounded by ancient buildings and dominated by the majestic Palazzo Vecchio (also called Palazzo della Signoria), this beautiful square has for centuries been the heart of Florentine life. Here the city's great historic and political events took place, here the whole course of events was shaped while, during its internal struggles, Florence grew to power and sent forth its culture to the world. The building, conceived as the seat of the Signoria, the governing body of the Republic, and probably designed by Arnolfo di Cambio, was constructed between 1298 and 1314. Extensions and modifications were made to it later by Buontalenti and by Vasari.

119

The Uffizi Gallery. - This imposing building, which has two parallel wings joined by an upper floor at the farther end, stands beside the Palazzo Vecchio and contains one of the greatest collections of paintings in the world. It was built by order of the Medici ruler Cosimo I and was intended to house the administrative offices of the State. The task of constructing it was given to Vasari, and documents of the time reveal that, to make room for it, no less than 234 private dwellings between the river Arno and Piazza della Signoria had to be expropriated. Among the buildings demolished was the church of San Pietro Scheraggio which, up till the 12th century, served as the meeting place for the city council. Construction of the Uffizi as an administrative building was completed in 1564, but in 1574 Grand Duke Francesco I decided to gather together the art treasures of his family, which were scattered in various palaces and villas. For this purpose he gave Buontalenti the task of transforming the open gallery on the building's upper floor into a long corridor lined with rooms. The early collection was enriched over the years through the unfailing interest in the arts shown by all members of the Medici family. The successors of the Medici, the House of Lorraine, happily proved eager to maintain this tradition. Indeed it was a member of this family, Leopoldo, who first opened the gallery to the public and put the task of ordering and caring for its collection in the hands of art experts.

Uffizi Gallery. - GIOTTO (?1267-1337): *Madonna in Glory.*

Uffizi Gallery. - Piero della Francesca (1416-1492): *Portrait of Federico da Montefeltro.*

Uffizi Gallery. - Paolo Uccello (c. 1396-1451): *The Battle of San Romano.*

Uffizi Gallery. - Masolino (1383-1447) and Masaccio (1401-1428): *Madonna and Child with Saint Anne.* Masolino was commissioned to do this work but after finishing the figures of Saint Anne and the Angels — except for the angel on the right, dressed in green — he left its completion to his pupil Masaccio, giving him a completely free hand.

Uffizi Gallery. - FILIPPO LIPPI (?1406-1469): *Madonna and Child with Angels.*

Uffizi Gallery. - MICHELANGELO BUONARROTI (1475-1564): *Holy Family.* Also known as the Doni Tondo because it was commissioned by the Doni family.

Uffizi Gallery. - LEONARDO DA VINCI (1452-1519): *Annunciation.*

Uffizi Gallery. - ANDREA MANTEGNA (1431-1506): *Adoration of the Magi.*

◀ Uffizi Gallery. - Above: SANDRO BOTTICELLI (1445-1510): *Spring.* Below: SANDRO
BOTTICELLI (1445-1510): *Birth of Venus.*

Santa Croce Basilica. - Standing on the former site of an older, smaller church of the Franciscan order, Santa Croce was begun in the middle of the 12th century and finished at the end of the 14th century. A masterpiece of Florentine Gothic architecture, it is usually attributed to Arnolfo di Cambio. The marble facade is a more recent addition by Nicolò Matas (1857-1863) while the bell-tower, which imitates the Gothic style, was designed by Gaetano Baccani in 1847.

Santa Croce Basilica. Interior. - Divided into three naves by graceful pillars and pointed Gothic arches, it has the open-beam ceiling common to all the Franciscan churches. At one time the walls were covered with frescoes by Giotto and his helpers; these would have come down to us except that in the 16th century Giorgio Vasari, commissioned by the Medici ruler Cosimo I with the task of rearranging the church, covered most of the frescoes with plaster, and placed altars of little merit along the walls. Many of Italy's most illustrious sons are buried here, and those whose actual tombs are elsewhere are commemorated by monuments, so that the church has become a national shrine.

Piazza Santa Maria Novella. - On this square, one of the largest and most beautiful in Florence, stands the Dominican Church of Santa Maria Novella with its striking marble facade. Designed in the Gothic style, the church was begun in 1279 by two friars of the Dominican order, Sisto di Firenze and Ristoro da Campi, and completed by another Dominican, Jacopo Talenti, who also built the church's graceful bell-tower. The harmonious facade in green and white marble was designed by Leon Battista Alberti, and erected between 1456 and 1470. The obelisk in front of the church and the identical one at the other end of the square mark the limits of the course around which a famous horse-and-carriage race was once held. The event, inspired by the ancient Roman chariot races, was introduced by Cosimo I in 1563.

Piazza San Lorenzo. - This picturesque and animated square lies a short way from the Cathedral in the heart of Florence's historic centre. Dominating the square's restricted space is the massive Church of San Lorenzo, surrounded by the stalls of the popular marketplace. The commission to build San Lorenzo, which was to be virtually the family church of the Medici, was given to Filippo Brunelleschi in 1421 by Giovanni Bicci de' Medici; it was completed in 1460 by Brunelleschi's pupil Antonio Manetti. It stands on the site of a famous ancient church which was consecrated in 393 by St. Ambrose, Bishop of Milan.

San Lorenzo. New Sacristy. - Created by Michelangelo, who received the commission from Cardinal Giulio de' Medici — later to become Pope Clement VII — this building was designed as a burial chapel for the Medici family; in it are interred the remains of Lorenzo the Magnificent and his brother Giuliano, plus those of Giuliano, Duke of Nemours, and Lorenzo, Duke of Urbino. In his design of the chapel, completely devoid of ostentation, Michelangelo expresses supreme universal values. The four statues which he created for the Medici tombs — Day and Night on one, Dawn and Dusk on the other — refer to the inexorable passage of time and approaching death; at the same time they divide each tomb into two parts, calling the viewer's attention to the centre of the sarcophagi from which the souls of the dead (represented by the statues of the two dukes) seem to issue forth and rise towards heaven. At the centre of the photo, on the wall in the background, is the tomb containing the remains of Lorenzo the Magnificent and his brother Giuliano, over which stand the statues of the Madonna, also by Michelangelo, and of the Saints Cosmas and Damian, the former by Montorsoli and the latter by Raffaello da Montelupo.

San Lorenzo. New Sacristy. - MICHELANGELO BUONARROTI (1475-1564): *Tomb of Lorenzo, Duke of Urbino.* The duke, grandson of Lorenzo the Magnificent, is depicted by Michelangelo in a contemplative pose with the statues of Dawn and Dusk at his feet.

San Lorenzo. New Sacristy. - Michelangelo Buonarroti (1475-1564). *Tomb of Giuliano, Duke of Nemours.* Michelangelo's statue of the Medici duke shows him wearing armour and carrying the commander's baton, symbol of the man of action; at his feet are the symbolic figures of Day and Night.

The Pitti Palace. - The historian Vasari recounts that « Messer Luca Pitti commissioned from Filippo (Brunelleschi) a magnificent palace outside the San Niccolò gate in Florence, in the place called Rucciano ». And in fact records show that on August 19, 1441, the governing body of Florence decided to grant Pitti, the Republic's renowned gonfalonier, a piece of land on the hill now occupied by the Boboli Gardens where he was to construct a new and more opulent home. Indeed, according to the popular tradition Pitti wanted a house so grandiose that its windows were to be as big as the doors of the Medici family's palace. Its construction, begun in about 1457, probably under the direction of Luca Fancelli, was discontinued in 1465 because of Pitti's part in an ill-fated plot against Piero de' Medici. Only the central section of the palace — including the three central arches which serve as doorways and the seven windows above them — had been completed. In 1550 Eleanor of Toledo, wife of the Grand Duke Cosimo I, acquired the palace for the Medici family and since Brunelleschi's plan had disappeared the duchess had new plans drawn up by Bartolomeo Ammanati. Between 1558 and 1577 the great courtyard, Ammanati's masterpiece, was constructed, but the building was still not completed. In 1620 Cosimo II had the front of the palace extended, adding three windows to each side; five more windows were added by Ferdinand II in 1640. Finally the wings on each side were constructed during the rule of the Lorraine family between 1764 and 1799. The interior of the palace, which has been greatly altered, contains nevertheless vivid reminders of the Savoys, who made the Pitti Palace their royal residence during the five years when Florence was the capital of Italy (1865-1870). In 1919 Victor Emmanuel II presented the palace to the State to house administrative offices and, more importantly, large art collections. Today the palace contains not only the Museo degli Argenti, or Treasure Museum, but also the Palatine Gallery, with its many outstanding paintings including the royal collection.

Palatine Gallery. - ANTHONY VAN DYCK (1559-1641). *Portrait of Cardinal Guido Bentivoglio.*

Palatine Gallery. - BARTOLOMEO ESTEBAN MURILLO (c. 1618-c. 1682): *Madonna and Child.*

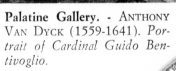

Palatine Gallery. - FILIPPO LIPPI (c. 1406-1469): *Madonna and Child.*

Ponte Santa Trinita. - This, the most majestic of the bridges over the Arno, was built by Bartolomeo Ammanati between 1567 and 1569. Under the influence of Michelangelo, Ammanati made it one of the finest bridges in Italian Renaissance architecture. Destroyed on August 4, 1944, during the Second World War, it was faithfully reconstructed in its original form, using mainly the original material recovered from the river.

Piazza Santo Spirito. - This picturesque square lies in the middle of the district on the far side of the river Arno, one of the oldest parts of Florence. At the end of the square stands one of the purest architectural expressions of the spirit of the early Renaissance: the church of Santo Spirito. Designed by Brunelleschi, who began work on it in 1444, it was completed by Antonio Manetti and Salvi D'Andrea in 1487 after Brunelleschi's death. The bell-tower to the left of the church is the work of Baccio d'Agnolo, while the cupola was built by Salvi D'Andrea to a design by Brunelleschi.

Ponte Vecchio. - The Ponte Vecchio, or « Old Bridge », is so called because it was the first bridge built across the Arno. Reconstructed several times, its present form is the work of Neri di Fioravante in 1345. Lining the bridge are the picturesque little goldsmiths' and silversmiths' shops which have become world-famous. In 1564, by order of Francesco I, Vasari built the passageway which crosses the bridge above the shops and links the Palazzo Vecchio on one side of the Arno with the Pitti Palace on the other.

Church of San Marco. - Attached to the Dominican priory, the church looks out over a wide square with a garden in the centre. The church was designed by Michelozzo in 1437, while the baroque facade was erected by Fra Gioacchino Pronti in 1870. The wooden door is the same one which in the 15th century resisted attempts by an angry mob to burn it down, enter the church and seize the controversial preacher and religious dictator Savonarola.

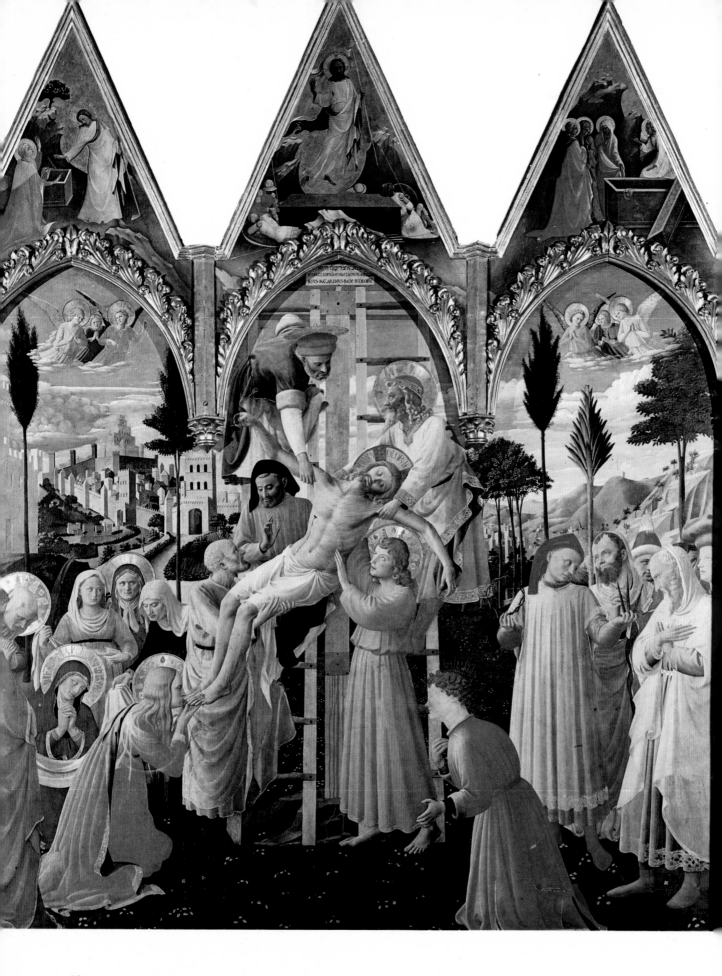

Gallery of the Accademia. - MICHEL-
ANGELO BUONARROTI (1475-1564):
David. In a contract dated August
16, 1501, the committee which
controlled Florence's cathedral, together with the city's gonfalonier,
Pier Soderini, commissioned Michelangelo to create a statue symbolising the liberty of the Commune
which was to be placed in front of
the Palazzo Vecchio. The artist had
to chisel his statue out of a block
of marble already badly marred by
Agostino di Duccio in 1464 in an
abandoned attempt to create a statue
for the outside of the Cathedral.
The damage done to the block made
it a difficult task, but as Vasari
recounts: « After examining it, Michelangelo conceived a figure which
might be created from the block
as the symbol for the Palazzo Vecchio. He then made a wax model
of a young David with his sling
in his hand — signifying that, just
as David had defended his people
and governed them justly, so should
the rulers of Florence defend their
city courageously and govern it
justly ». The young Michelangelo —
he was 26 when he began the David — worked at a relentless pace
and in September 1504 the statue
was placed on the steps of the
Palazzo Vecchio. Here it remained
until 1873 when, to protect it from
damage by the weather, it was transferred to a specially prepared stand
in the Gallery of the Accademia.
The dynamic tension in every part
of this magnificent work, the proud,
handsome face looking confidently
towards the foe, the strongly defined
anatomical features with the muscles
ready for action, the supreme human
dignity of the whole statue, all show
clearly what a great artist Michelangelo was, even at this early stage
of his career.

San Marco Museum. - FRA GIO-
VANNI called BEATO ANGELICO
[GUIDO DI PIETRO TOSINI] (1400-
1455): *Deposition.*

Piazza San Firenze. - In the background of this typical Florentine square stands the slim bell-tower of the Badia Church, with the more distant shape of the Cathedral's huge cupola outlined beside it. But what dominates the square more than anything else is the severe mass of the Bargello, whose construction dates back to 1254. First occupied by city government leaders including the « Capitano del Popolo » (the magistrate acting in the people's interests) and the « Podestà » (the head of government), it became in the 15th century the headquarters of the chief of police, known as the « Bargello », from which the building takes its name. The bell in its tower is called the « Montanina » because it was carried off by the Florentines from the castle of Montale; it was formerly rung when the judges began their sittings in the courts of law, or to indicate the hours in which citizens were prohibited from carrying arms on the streets, or else to announce that a prisoner had been put in the pillory at the foot of the tower (the use of the pillory continued until 1848). Today the Bargello is a National Museum housing a collection of sculpture and paintings.

Palazzo del Bargello. Courtyard. - Surrounded on three sides by arcades, with the imposing stairway designed by Neri di Fioravante on the other, this courtyard is full of memories of the past. Here, beside the well, stood the gallows, while nearby in what is now the armoury was the torture-chamber; the list of those who suffered and died in this room includes such illustrious names as the Albizi, the Peruzzi and the Strozzi, families who conspired against the government of Florence.

National Museum. - This museum is housed in the Palazzo del Bargello, and contains above all a collection of Tuscan sculpture from the Middle Ages and the Renaissance. The photographs show the different interpretations by two artists of the same subject: « The Young David ». The version on the left is by Donato de' Bardi, called Donatello (c. 1382-1466), and that on the right by Andrea di Cione, called Verrocchio (1436-1488).

PISA

Pisa is famous above all for its group of magnificent monuments, the Baptistry, the Cathedral, the Leaning Tower and the Camposanto, which stand together on the splendid green lawns of the Piazza dei Miracoli (« Field of Miracles »). This complex of buildings, outlined by their black and white marble, were planned to stand at the centre of a Pisa envisaged as the capital of a powerful maritime state and the centre of its empire. And indeed during the 12th century, Pisa had established itself as an important maritime republic, whose flag with its cross could be seen flying in Palestine and Turkey, in Sardinia, Naples and Amalfi. Unfortunately, internal strife led to its early downfall: the Genoese, taking advantage of this weakness, defeated the Pisans in the disastrous battle of Meloria on 6 April 1284, and the grandeur of the Pisan republic came to an end.

Pisa is built on the banks of the River Arno, which flows into the sea nearby. In fact the fortifications along its banks in many cases serve as buttresses for the adjacent buildings, with their typical design inspired by Vasari. On the same banks stand the Chiesetta della Spina (« Church of the Thorn »), so tiny and exquisite that it seems the work of a goldsmith. Here the last farewells were said to adventurous Pisans who embarked on the waters of the Arno to sail down to the sea. After its downfall and later conquest by the Florentines, Pisa remained for long in a state of undisturbed mediocrity, protected by the Medici, rulers of Florence, to dream of its former greatness. But its fame was kept alive by the fact that it was the birthplace of Galileo, by its ancient and distinguished university, and by its school called the « Scuola Normale », so that it became widely known as a centre of learning where in the 19th century some of Italy's most illustrious scholars studied.

The Cathedral and Baptistry seen from the Leaning Tower. - In the foreground is the cupola, obviously of Oriental inspiration, which crowns the Cathedral at the point where its four arms meet. The graceful circle of Gothic arch motifs running round the base of the cupola was added in the second half of the 14th century. In the background: the Baptistry, which like the Cathedral is surmounted by a cupola covered with lead sheeting. However, as can be seen more clearly in the photo on the preceding page, only part of the Baptistry's cupola has this lead covering; the remainder is tiled. The Pisans justify this apparent oddity by explaining that their ancestors were forced to use the lead from the cupola as war material during their final heroic struggle for liberty against the Florentines, the siege of 1509 which ended in the surrender of the city.

The Duomo. - Although its construction took a century and a half to complete, Pisa's cathedral has an architectural unity so complete that every element, structural or decorative, plays its aesthetic part, and the building as a whole attains functional perfection. Dedicated to the Virgin Mary it stands on the wide green lawns of the magnificent Piazza dei Miracoli. It was begun in 1603 to a design by Buscheto Pisano (born about 1035), a little known and much debated architect who must nevertheless have enjoyed great prestige in his own time, judging from the fact that his successors in the long and difficult task of constructing the Cathedral followed so closely his original conception. Construction was interrupted in 1095 but resumed in 1099 and completed in 1118, the year in which Pope Gelasius consecrated the Cathedral. However, the facade, designed by Maestro Rainaldo, was erected in the 13th century when the length of the nave was extended. The Cathedral became the progenitor of the Pisan Romanesque architectural style, whose influence can be seen not only in churches in Tuscany, Corsica and Sardinia but as far away as Dalmatia and Apulia.

The Leaning Tower. - The world-wide fame of the Leaning Tower of Pisa, where Galileo conducted his noted experiments on falling bodies, is kept alive by periodic alarms which usually follow the regular measurements taken to check its movement. But the tower, which stands at the eastern end of the complex of buildings in the Piazza dei Miracoli, in perfect harmony with their style, is also a superbly decorative work of art. Its foundations were laid in 1173, to a design by Bonanno Pisano with the collaboration of Guglielmo, though in this initial phase the construction reached only the third tier before being abandoned because the ground level on the southern side had subsided seriously. The tower's cylindrical design was not a new idea, but the colonnaded passages which encircle the white marble structure make it extremely original. The repetition of its arch motifs not only unites it stylistically to the Cathedral, but seems to reduce its mass through the resultant effects of light and shade. The theory that the tower's inclination from the vertical was deliberately planned by its builders is without foundation. History shows that several unsuccessful attempts to complete it were made by architects of proven ability; but not until the middle of the 14th century did Tommaso, son of Andrea Pisano, put the finishing touch to the bell-chamber at its summit.

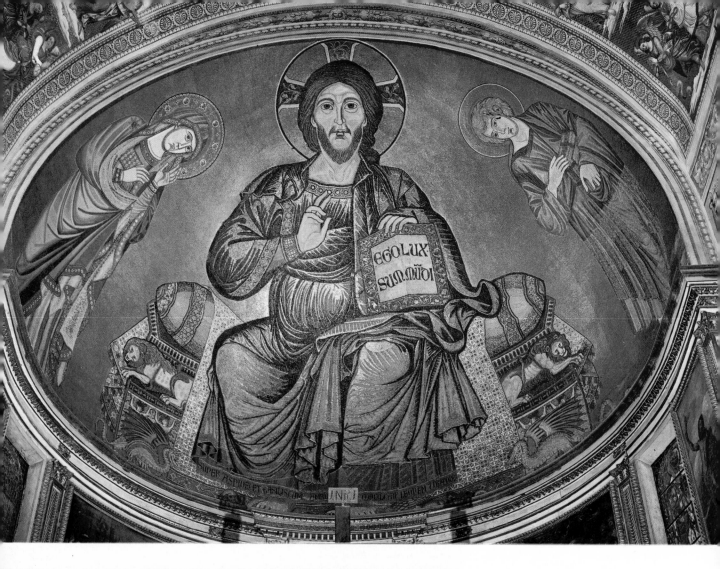

The Cathedral. Interior. - *Mosaic in the apse.* - The mosaic, which depicts Christ enthroned between Our Lady and St. John the Evangelist, was done in the first quarter of the 14th century. Though clearly within the Byzantine tradition, an attempt can be seen in the garments to suggest the volume of the bodies.

The Cathedral. Interior. - GIO-VANNI PISANO (fl. 1265-1317): *Slaughter of the Innocents* (detail of the *Pulpit*). - Giovanni's mastery of the sculptor's art reaches its apex in this panel. His anguished rendering gives full expression to the unleashed fury of the soldiers and the desperate resistance of the weeping mothers, crouching before the imperious, Michelangelesque gesture of Herod.

The Cathedral. Interior. - In the central nave, inundated with light from its ample windows, the black lines along the walls and on the pillars of the women's gallery lead the eye towards the apse. In the church is the fine pulpit by Giovanni Pisano. Sculpted between 1302 and 1310, broken up during a fire in 1595 and reassembled in 1926, it is the most ornate of the pulpits by the Pisan school. Hanging in the nave is the 16th century chandelier by Vincenzo Possenti whose movements are said to have led Galileo to discover his law on the oscillation of pendulums.

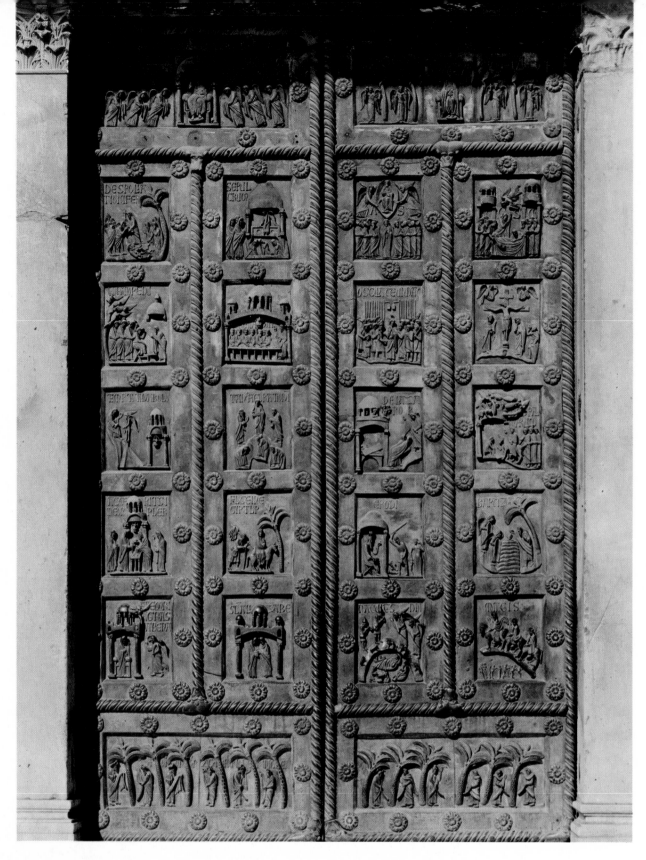

The Cathedral. - Bonanno Pisano (active from 1174 to 1186): *Bronze door.* -
Bonanno decorated the door, cast in 1180, in a personal and highly poetic way,
creating vigorous little figures of a Byzantine elegance. The twenty panels depict
episodes from the life of Christ, and below them are the figures of twelve prophets.
The artist added an explanatory title to each scene.

The Baptistry. - Standing on the green of the field like an enormous crown, the Baptistry was designed by the architect Diotisalvi in a style aimed at complementing the facade of the Cathedral beside it. Construction was begun in August, 1152, when Pisa was at the height of its power, but the project was interrupted so many times that it is difficult to know how closely the original plan was followed. However, its fundamentally Romanesque structure remains clearly visible, despite the Gothic decoration added later to the upper part of the building.

The Baptistry. Interior. - In the centre of the Baptistry, on a base three steps high, is the baptismal font, its octagonal form completely in harmony with the circular building itself. It was designed by Guido Bigarelli da Como, and completed in 1246. In the centre of the font is a column with Byzantine capitals which supports a modern bronze statue of St. John the Baptist by Italo Griselli. Behind it, on the left, is the famous hexagonal pulpit by Nicola Pisano. The pulpit is essentially Tuscan in style, and represents a break with preceding tradition, not only in the hexagonal form which makes it stand out from the wall. In fact, the pulpit is a masterpiece which inspired a completely new school of sculptors and marked a new phase in the history of art.

The Camposanto. - Pisa's famous cemetery is called the Camposanto, or « Holy Ground », because it contains earth brought from the hill of Calvary by the archbishop Lanfranchi during the Crusades, and used to consecrate the cemetery. It stands alongside the Cathedral, Baptistry and Leaning Tower. The Camposanto building, designed by Giovanni di Simione, was begun in 1272 and continued despite Pisa's political and economic vicissitudes. It was completed in its present form in the second half of the 15th century: a huge rectangular cloister lined with a series of delicately carved mullioned windows in the Gothic style. The Camposanto contains many artistic masterpieces, including the great fresco cycles along its walls, works of sculpture by the Pisan school, and various sarcophagi, most of which belong to the Hellenistic period of Greek art. Unfortunately, it suffered irreparable damage during the Second World War when exploding grenades set fire to the roof: the fire caused many frescoes to crumble and come away from the walls.

Camposanto. *The Triumph of Death* (detail of the left-hand part). The colours of this great cycle of paintings, by an unknown artist, were altered by a fire in the Camposanto, but it is still the most important and striking of the works here. In the photograph can be seen a detail, depicting a group of riders, three of whom are identified by popular tradition with the Emperor Ludovik the Bavarian, and the Pisan political leaders, Uguccione della Faggiola and Castruccio Castracani.

Camposanto. - GIOVANNI PISANO (c. 1250 - c. 1320): *Madonna and Child.*

Standing on a ridge of hills, the red-brick buildings of Siena are surrounded by country which varies from the scrub at the beginning of the Maremma zone to the clay soils at the foot of the Amiata range. The city has retained intact its medieval appearance, almost untouched by the ravages of time. Its houses, standing on steep slopes, are supported by arches, and patches of green have crept in wherever possible between the churches and other buildings. Siena is a series of winding streets and alleys, of ascents and descents full of picturesque little surprises for the visitor. From the narrow side-streets, unexpected glimpses can be had of the heart of the city: the reddish-brown, shell-shaped square called Piazza del Campo, splendidly framed by the Palazzo Pubblico, with the Mangia Tower standing out against the blue of the sky, and the other buildings, with their graceful three-mullioned windows and balconies. Nearby is the imposing mass of the Cathedral, lightened by its alternating bands of black and white marble, a reminder of the time when the city-state of Siena was at the height of its power. Siena in fact, between the 11th and 12th centuries, became a city of considerable importance, so much so that at one point it seemed almost greater than its nearby rival, Florence. But in the 16th century the Florentine Cosimo de' Medici conquered the city, despite its inhabitants' retreat to Montalcino in a last, desperate bid to resist Florence's superior military strength. After this defeat, Siena was cut off from the more important commercial routes and became part of the territory of the Florentine grand dukes. But its inhabitants retained a fierce loyalty towards their city, a loyalty still alive today, as can be seen during the Palio, the famous horse-race run every year. As one writer has remarked: « The Palio is the people's festival, in which all its sympathies and personal feelings are expressed ».

Fonte Gaia. - The fountain in the centre of Piazza del Campo was given its name, which means « gay fountain », after the celebrations held for its inauguration in 1419. It was formerly embellished with fine bas-reliefs by Jacopo della Quercia, depicting scenes from the Old and New Testaments. The original works, damaged by time, were removed and replaced by copies at the end of the 19th century. The originals are preserved today in the Palazzo Pubblico.

Cappella di Piazza. - Designed by Domenico di Agostino, it was built in 1353 as an act of thanksgiving to commemorate the end of the terrible plague of 1348, which had claimed 30,000 dead in Siena alone and marked the beginning of the city's decline. Distinguished by the whiteness of its marble from the Gothic-style Palazzo Pubblico, the chapel originally consisted of columns — between which were statues by Sienese artists depicting various saints — covered by a simple roof. The Renaissance arches and decoration were added in 1468 by Antonio Federighi, who also supervised the reconstruction of the roof.

Palazzo Pubblico. - The combination of solemnity and elegance makes this building the most original product of the Italian Gothic style. Its beauty lies in the facade, slightly curved as if to meet and complement the spacious, sloping square in front of it; in the two contrasting colours of the bricks; in the delicate, three-mullioned windows; and in the tall, slim tower on the left, known as the Mangia Tower, standing out against the sky like a naked sword, symbol of Siena's liberty. Designed by Agostino di Giovanni and Agnolo di Ventura, the Palazzo Pubblico was built between 1297 and 1343 as the seat of the « Government of Nine ». High on the the taller central section of the building is the name of Christ in the emblem of San Bernardino, painted by Battista di Niccolò da Padova in 1425. The Medici coat-of-arms was affixed in 1560 after the conquest of Siena.

Palazzo Pubblico. Interior. -
AMBROGIO LORENZETTI (fl.
1324-1334): *The Effects of
Good Government in the City.*
Here, in the Sala della Pace,
is the largest fresco cycle of a
non-religious nature surviving
from this period. This section
contains a vision of 14th-cen-
tury Siena, with its streets and
buildings, groups of knights
on horseback and girls-absorb-
ed in a graceful dance.

Palazzo Pubblico. Interior. - SI-
MONE MARTINI (1283-1344):
*Guido Riccio da Fogliano at
the Siege of Montemassi.* Detail of the fresco in the Sala
del Mappamondo. The figure
of the military leader stands
in striking isolation against the
background of the army camp.

Palazzo Pubblico. Interior. - SIMONE MARTINI (1283-1344): *La Maestà*. This work, depicting the Madonna and Child surrounded by angels and the patron saints of Siena, recalls the painting by Martini's famous predecessor, Duccio, now in the Museo dell'Opera del Duomo. Martini's Maestà is noteworthy for its colours and fluidity of line.

Church of San Domenico. - An imposing brick structure whose oldest part dates back to 1254, its original design was based on that of the churches of the Cistercian monastic order. A century and a half later, it was extended with the building of the lower church. A tall bell-tower with spire was also erected, though this was later reduced in height, the spire being replaced by battlements. Inside, in the Cappella delle Volte, is the famous fresco with a portrait of St. Catherine, painted by her disciple, Andrea Vanni. The body of St. Catherine is preserved in another chapel, which has frescoes by Sodoma.

The Palio - The spirit of Siena cannot be understood by anyone who has not
seen its famous traditional horse-race, the Palio. The race is not an artificial historical
re-enactment, but a tradition which has been alive for centuries and has its roots
in Siena's everyday life. It is held in Piazza del Campo, the square in the centre
of the city, and excites strong partisan feelings, since the horses represent the
various ancient quarters of the city, each named after a bird or animal, a battle-
symbol or a natural object. The Palio is run twice a year, on July 2 and August 16,
and is preceded by a procession which is perhaps the most spectacular element
for the visitor. The procession is led by a herald carrying the black and
white flag of Siena; he is followed by others in costume, who stand for the
various powers of the ancient Sienese Republic. Then come the representatives of
the 10 quarters whose horses will take part in the Palio: the horses are drawn
by lot, so that some quarters have already been eliminated. The procession has
its climax when the standard-bearers of the various quarters come together to give
a skilful and spectacular exhibition, twirling their brightly coloured flags and tossing
them in the air. After them come the representatives of the seven quarters whose
horses are not racing, and then the « Carroccio », the carriage which once
bore Siena's standard into battle and today carries the « Palio » itself, the banner
which is the prize for the race. Around the Carroccio are the representatives of the
six quarters which were abolished for having incited an uprising during the race
on July 2, 1675. When the procession is over comes the event for which the
Sienese have been waiting, the race itself: three minutes of frantic excitement
followed by the flush of triumph for the winner and his supporters.

The Cathedral. - An imposing mass dominating the square but lightened by the different colours of its marble exterior, this is one of the finest Italian cathedrals in the Romano-Gothic style. The combination of the earlier Romanesque and the later Gothic styles is due to the length of time taken to construct the cathedral: it was begun in 1196, but not completed until 1397. The facade, designed by Giovanni Pisano, honours the Virgin Mary, to whom Siena dedicated itself on the eve of the Battle of Montaperti. The traditionally static Gothic form of the facade is animated by the deep-set portals and the vigorous sculptural groups. The lower part is covered with scenes from the Old Testament and the upper part with scenes from the New Testament, while the image of the Virgin Mary in the rose-window dominates the whole facade. The cathedral's bell-tower, built on the foundations of an older tower, is in the Lombard-Pisan style; the greater number of openings towards the top of the tower create an effect of ever-increasing slenderness and fragility. Like the exterior, the interior of the cathedral is dressed with alternating bands of black and white marble. It contains innumerable artistic masterpieces, from the scenes carved on the floor, to the pulpit by Nicola Pisano, created in collaboration with his son Giovanni, and the spacious Gothic vaults. In the background, on the right, can be seen a series of large arches, the beginnings of a project never realised: in 1340 construction was interrupted by the desire to emulate Florence's famous cathedral. The Sienese wanted to erect a vast edifice of which the part already built would have been only the cross-vault, but abandoned it after the plague epidemic of 1348 and resultant economic crisis.

UMBRIA AND MARCHE

At the centre of the Italian peninsula is a region which is unique for many geographical and historical reasons: Umbria. It is a region whose peculiar tranquillity one can feel walking along the shores of Lake Trasimeno, and looking at the valleys, and the villages and houses scattered across the Umbrian hills. Many of these are built in remote and solitary places, and writers have remarked on the individualism in the Umbrian character which led, for reasons of defence or of mystic fervour, to the selection of such lonely sites. Monasteries were built by the various religious orders in magnificent positions looking down on the panorama. And the Romans, the free commeunes and the lords of the Papal States constructed strongholds and fortresses at strategic points. These buildings, the remains of a dynamic past, have become an integral part of the Umbrian countryside.

The region's history is lost in the mists of time. When Rome was still no more than a village, Perugia, which was then the last outpost of the Etruscan people on the border with Latium, had no less than seven massive city-gates at its entrances. The oldest evidence of the life of the ancient Umbrians was furnished by the discovery of the « Gubbio Tablets », which contain writings in the Umbrian language using letters of both the Etruscan and Latin alphabets, and have thus permitted scholars to form some idea of the customs of this people before it came under the domination of the Romans.

In the 3rd century B. C. the Umbrians were conquered by the Romans and became their faithful allies, so much so that when Hannibal, after the victorious battle of Trasimeno, thought to gain them over to his side as he had with other regions, he found the gates of the city of Spoleto barred in his face. Spoleto was also the city which in the early Middle Ages became the seat of the Longobard duchy, destined to dominate for a time the entire region. In Umbria too the first free communes were formed, cities which were in an almost continuous state of war between each other and were often torn by fierce internal faction fighting. In the 16th century, Umbria became part of the Papal States, and it remained so until 1860 when the citizens of Perugia rose and seized the Paoline fortress.

There are two outstanding aspects of Umbrian life between the 13th century and the 16th century: its culture, and the part it took in Catholic reforms. In 1307 a flourishing university was founded at Perugia, and in 1472 the first edition of Dante's *Divine Comedy* was published at Foligno: two major events in the history of civilisation. St. Benedict of Norcia and, later, St. Francis of Assisi had determining roles in the formation of the doctrine of the Catholic Church. Equally active were Umbria's military captains, two of the most important being Gattamelata, immortalised by Donatello's statue of him at Padua, and Baglioni, who led and betrayed the Florentines during the famous siege of Florence in 1529. Its artists too, though they felt strongly the influences of Florence, Rome, Siena and Venice, gave a particular character to their work which can be seen in the paintings of the last important members of the Umbrian School, Perugino and Pinturicchio.

Before its conquest by the Papal States, all the cities of Umbria had been active in religious building and in public works: evidence of this can be seen in the churches and monasteries and in the palaces built for government leaders which proliferate throughout the region. The discovery of Umbria's rich heritage is thus as rewarding as it is demanding. Not only its more famous cities should be seen: Etruscan Perugia, the mystic city of Assisi, mountainous Gubbio, Orvieto with its Gothic aspect, Spoleto with its formidable fortress, Foligno, Terni with its industry. Also the smaller towns merit a visit: Città di Castello, Todi, Città della Pieve, Gualdo Tadino, Umbertide, Deruta, Amelia, Narni, Sangemini, Norcia, Cascia, Montefaloco, Spello. The region's fascination has been felt not only by the ancient poets but also by modern artists. The springs known as the Fonti del Clitunno are the subject of a celebrated painting by Corot; Byron also wrote about them, as did Carducci in his famous ode in 1876. Nor should one forget, among other things, the Cascata delle Marmore, an artificial waterfall built by the Romans in 271 A. D., or the romantic lake of Piediluco.

Slightly larger than Umbria, with mountains which slope down to gentle hills and thence to the beaches of the Adriatic Sea, is Italy's other central region, the Marche. The Marche is different from other Italian regions in that it has never had a major centre to co-ordinate its cultural and economic activities. The explanation for this odd fact is undoubtedly to be found above all in the region's topography. Its valleys down which flow streams of various sizes but all historically important — including the Foglia, the Metauro, the Esino, the Chienti and the Tronto — are not linked by communications routes, but rather slope down separately to the Adriatic Sea.

Ancona, the chief city in the region, has never had particularly important links with the other cities, nor has it ever had a determining role in the cultural and economic development of the Marche. The inhabitants of the Marche have always felt the attraction of a quite different centre, that is, Rome, to which the region was linked by two Roman roads built during the consular period: the Via Salaria and Via Flaminia. Rome was the city which most profited from the genius of the Marche's greatest citizens: from the painter Raphael to the architect Bramante and the popes Sextus V and Pius IX.

Urbino perhaps was the only city which, in the second half of the 15th century, almost aspired to the role of capital of the region. This city has been called the fruit of a cultural unity achieved by the perfect fusion of different elements: the wise prince as governor and administrator of his people, the urban architect Luciano Laurano who organised the spaces in the city and their functions, the painter Piero della Francesca who saw in painting a form of knowledge whereby men could understand themselves and act to control their destiny. Urbino was to extend this sense of order throughout the region, from Gubbio to Senigallia, from San Leo to Pesaro and Cagli, infusing with it the many buildings and monuments which still today testify to Urbino's power and distinguish this northern part of the Marche from the south.

In fact, the region never had even an appearance of political unity until it was incorporated whole into the Papal States. It has always been a « marca » or « march », a Germanic word meaning border. It was a border territory for the Piceni tribes, for the Gauls, the Romans, the Goths and the Ostrogoths, the Byzantines and the Longobards, and again later for the nobles who, with the support of popes or emperors, became the rulers of its city-states, such as the Montefeltro, Verano and Malatesta families. It is true, however, that the « march », the real border territory, was the southern part of the region, the areas around Fermo, Ancona and Ascoli. In the northern part, a group of small dominions was created, so that until the middle of the 15th century the Marche was virtually divided into two parts. The northern and southern sections were unified only when the region came under the Papal States.

One must be familiar with the countryside of the Marche, with its tapestry of greens and browns, to arrive at an understanding of the strange beauty of Leopardi's poetry; the « interminable spaces » about which Leopardi wrote must be seen in the context of the ancient oaks and the ricks of straw standing near the farmhouses of the region. Its valleys, sloping down towards the sea from the Apennines, contain cities which are very different: Pesaro, surrounded by hills with their castles and villas, of a subtle beauty which inspired one of Giovanni Bellini's masterpieces, and a serenity whose echoes can be heard in the music of Gioacchino Rossini; Urbino, the city-palace created for Federico da Montefeltro by the architect Laurana; Fabriano, famous for its paper-mills; Senigallia, with its wide sandy shore; Iesi, birthplace of Frederick II of Swabia and of Gian Battista Pergolesi; Ancona, standing on the Adriatic Sea on which it depends for its livelihood; Recanati, indissolubly linked to the memory of its great poet, Leopardi; Loreto, with its celebrated sanctuary, one of the most imposing monuments of the Renaissance; Camerino, with its centuries-old university; the turreted city of Ascoli, which has managed to amalgamate the influences of both northern and southern Italy. However, despite the individual natures of its cities, the Marche has an unmistakeable atmosphere which makes a harmonious whole of its local differences, from the Apennines down to the sea.

PERUGIA

The city of Perugia, once protected by a circle of walls built by the Etruscans, lies in the heart of the Umbria region and dominates the surrounding plain from the hills on which it is built. It is equally famous for its many fine churches, and for its modern factories whose products are known throughout the world. Built as it is on a group of hills, Perugia is a city of steep streets and of stairways, dating from many different epochs. In the centre of the city, standing on one of the finest squares in Italy and recalling Perugia's period as a free commune, is a splendid group of monuments: the Palazzo dei Priori, which contains the most important collection of Umbrian paintings in existence; the 13th-century fountain with its sculptural works by Nicola and Giovanni Pisano; and the cathedral. But apart from the monuments testifying to its glorious past, Perugia today is acquiring a more and more international atmosphere. Arabs, Africans and Asians can be seen walking through its streets and squares, and one can hear snatches of conversation in almost every language in the world. This is a result of the ever-increasing fame of Perugia's University for Foreign Students, where international unity seems a reality and the barriers between nations no longer exist. Alongside students from the Common Market countries, there are Poles, Hungarians, Czechoslovakians, Yugoslavians and Rumanians, as well as students from African and Asian countries. The students find a ready welcome among the people of Perugia who have a strong, resolute character, perhaps inherited from their Etruscan forebears and tempered by centuries of fierce opposition to outside domination. This sense of independence led to the establishment of Perugia as a free commune which, for its form of government and the length of its duration, can be compared in importance with the communes of Florence and Siena.

Fontana Maggiore. - This fountain, also called the Fontana di Piazza, consists of a large basin with a smaller concentric basin above it, and a bronze bowl above this again; it is Perugia's most important public monument from the 13th century. Constructed under the direction of the designer, Fra Bevignate, it is decorated with sculptural works by Nicola and Giovanni Pisano. The lower part has 50 mirrors with bas-reliefs, including allegorical figures of the months and the sciences and episodes from the sacred history of Rome and from Aesop's fables. The 24 mirrors of the upper pool are not decorated but are separated by statues of saints (among them St. Paul, St. Laurence, St. Herculaneum, St. Benedict and St. Maurice) and historical figures. The bronze bowl at the top of the fountain is by the goldsmith Rosso, a native of Perugia. Above the basin is a group of three nymphs by Giovanni Pisano.

GUBBIO. Palazzo dei Consoli. - One of the most important civil buildings remaining in Umbria from the Middle Ages, the Palazzo dei Consoli occupies a whole side of the square and overshadows the streets on either side. The unity of its design suggests that it is the work of a single architect, and in fact it is thought to have been erected by Gattapone, a native of Gubbio, between 1332 and 1346. Gubbio's traditional Corsa dei Ceri, a race in which teams of men carry huge church-candles, 10 or 15 ft. high, has its start each year in front of this building.

SPOLETO. The Cathedral. - Spoleto, standing below its imposing 14th century fortress, is a city whose history goes back three thousand years. Once the centre of a Longobard duchy, it retains intact today its medieval appearance. It is thus an ideal site for its centre of late medieval studies and for the regular cultural and artistic events, famous throughout the world, which are held here. Cordoned off from the street, the facade of the Cathedral can be seen in all its spectacular beauty. Its Romanesque lines are reminiscent of the church of San Ruffino at Assisi, though the cathedral has been extended and altered on several occasions. The Renaissance-style portico was built by Ambrogio di Antonio da Milano around 1490, and in the same period the spire was added to the bell-tower, originally constructed in the 12th century.

Seen in the distance, from the other side of the valley, Assisi is visible as a large grey mark on the side of Mount Subasio. As one approaches the city, the vague mark resolves into the clear outline of houses, towers and churches. One thing perhaps remains the same, whether one is far away or close to the city: the colour of Assisi, somewhere between pink and grey, a mixture of chalk and mother-of-pearl. Little can be added to what has already been written over the centuries about Assisi, one of the most celebrated places in the world. Suffice to say that it gave birth to St. Francis, and that St. Francis in turn inspired Giotto and the Basilica of St. Francis at Assisi – and that in this great artist and in this magnificent church lie the beginnings of Italy's incomparable art. Italy's greatest artists came to Assisi – Cimabue, Giotto and the followers of the Roman artist Pietro Cavallini, besides Pietro Lorenzetti and Simone Martini, from Siena. This is the city where less than 30 years ago the hostilities of the Second World War halted almost miracu-

lously. It is a city where the creeping jungle of concrete, spreading across the entire Italian peninsula, seems reluctant to enter. It has been called the « Citadel of God » and a New Jerusalem, in which art, nature and the faith come together in a peaceful accord worthy of St. Francis. At Assisi, there is an air of freshness and tranquillity rarely to be found in our unquiet society, a tranquillity which derives not only from the sublime religious moments in its history but also from humble everyday things: the swallows which make their nests in the church of San Damiano, the turtle-doves of the Porziuncola chapel, the tiny garden of the Church of Santa Chiara, and nearby the veiled nuns of the order of Santa Chiara who make mysterious beckoning signs from behind the grating of their convent. You may go to Assisi to pray to St. Francis, or to see the frescoes by Giotto. But whatever your reason, as has been justly observed before now, you run the serious risk of being seized by an uncontrollable desire to become a saint.

Basilica of St. Francis. - The spiritual heart of Assisi and of Italy, the basilica consists of two churches built one above the other. According to the traditional story, the architect was a monk, Frate Elia, a native of Assisi, to whom in 1228 Simone di Pucciarello made a gift of the ground on which the church and monastery were to be built. However, experts believe it more probable that the basilica was designed by an artist familiar with the French Gothic style of architecture, whose inspiration can be seen in the exterior, but mindful also of the older Romanesque tradition, identifiable in the spacious design of the interior. The basilica's foundation stone was laid by Pope Gregory IX on July 17, 1228, the day after the canonisation of St. Francis. The project went ahead so rapidly that within two years the body of the saint could be transferred to the as yet uncompleted church. A serious obstacle was created, however, by the controversy provoked by the so-called « zealous » members of the Franciscan order, who objected to the construction of such a lavish church in honour of the saint who had exalted the blessedness of poverty. As a result, the basilica was not completed until 1253.

Basilica of St. Francis. Lower Church. - SIMONE MARTINI (c. 1283-1344): *Santa Chiara*. Painted with great spiritual insight, this idealised portrait of the mystical companion of St. Francis is one of the most poetic works left to us by the Gothic school of painting.

Basilica of St. Francis. Lower Church. - CIMABUE (active between 1272 and 1301): *Madonna and Child with St. Francis*. The arrival at Assisi of this great painter, shortly to be followed by other celebrated artists, marks the beginning of the artistic experience which was to result in the regeneration of art. Cimabue's portrait of St. Francis is a masterly interpretation in which the saint's exaltation of poverty is given full expression.

Basilica of St. Francis. Upper Church. - GIOTTO (c. 1267-1337): *The Gift of the Cloak.* This is one of the 28 stories of St. Francis covering the walls of the upper church, painted by the master between 1296 and 1300. Unfortunately the frescoes are in such poor condition that there are sections very difficult to see, which is perhaps what has led some critics to doubt the attribution of all of them to Giotto. However, given the unified conception of the whole cycle, the revolutionary principles of composition, the inventive genius in perspective and three-dimensional projection, and the brilliant design to be found in each scene, it seems certain that the frescoes must be attributed to a single genius — that is, to Giotto. Worth noting in the fresco reproduced here are the compassionate gesture of St. Francis, the impoverished knight bowing slightly in deference, and the entirely natural behaviour of the horse, which is bending its head towards the ground, seeking a blade of grass. In no work of art prior to Giotto had nature, the landscape itself, seemed such a direct participant in the actions of man.

Basilica of St. Francis. Lower Church. - Giotto (1267-1337): *St. Francis expels the Evil Spirits from Arezzo.*

Santa Chiara. - Begun in 1257 and consecrated in 1265, this church contains the remains of St. Clare, the first and most important heroine of the Franciscan movement. On the facade, the Subasio marble of various colours in alternating bands creates a pictoric effect: the elements which stand out are the gabled portal, with its false porch, and the splendid rose-window. But the most noteworthy feature of the church are the flying buttresses, the soaring supports on each side of the church. Those on the right are bricked in: behind them are the convent, cloister and garden of the Poor Clares. The three buttresses on the left, which remain open, give an impression of lightness and grace.

Santa Chiara. Interior. - *Crucifix of St. Damian.* A panel painted by an unknown artist in the 12th century, in a somewhat rustic and archaic version of the Byzantine style. This is the crucifix which according to tradition spoke to St. Francis in the church of St. Damian.

ORVIETO

Orvieto is built on the spacious top of a hill formed from volcanic rock with sheer cliffs dropping into the valley of the Paglia River below, which the city overlooks. The city has many fine buildings from the 12th and 13th centuries, and is dominated by the imposing mass of its Duomo, which still retains its impressive medieval appearance. Indeed, it is impossible to talk about Orvieto without becoming involved in the discussion of this church, which is considered by some « the most beautiful Gothic cathedral in the world ». The famous cathedral continues to arouse controversy, and the latest dispute was over its bronze doors, recently made and erected by the modern sculptor Emilio Greco. The history of the city itself is full of stories of bitter divisions and feuds between families, which led to the formation of factions and involved the towns nearby as well in an endless series of insults, fights and vendettas. It is a story which resembles that of the Florentine families, the Cerchi and the Donati. At Orvieto the names were different — Monaldeschi and Filippeschi — but the political reasons for the feud were the same: the struggle between the ancient medieval parties, the Guelfs and the Ghibellines, to which was later added the internal struggle within the Guelf party itself. This dissension continued in Orvieto until the city came under the rule of the Papal States. However, the people always managed to unite in their most critical moments, and Orvieto was the only city apart from Florence which resisted the invasion of the French king, Charles VIII, at the end of the 15th century. Orvieto is a city of warm colours, to be seen in the brick and tuff, a volcanic stone abundantly used in its buildings. It is also a city which reflects the quiet but constant struggle of man to conserve more ancient beauties in the face of the inexorable march of progress.

THE DUOMO. - This is one of Italy's most outstanding architectural masterpieces, and the fact that it was built over a period of centuries does nothing to detract from its splendour. It was begun by Pope Nicholas IV in 1290 on the site of a former cathedral. The name of its designer is uncertain, but it is known that a monk called Fra Bevignate da Perugia was in charge of its construction in the 14th century.

The Cathedral. Interior. - The large, well-lit interior is divided into three naves by a series of ten columns and two pillars with finely sculpted capitals. An impressive effect of perspective is created by the fact that the capitals of the last columns have been lowered and the floor of the church raised towards the apse; the alternating bands of black and white marble on the walls and columns add to this effect. On the advice of Maderno in 1619, hoops were put around the base of some of the columns — such as the one on the left in the photo — because they were in danger of collapsing. Inside the cathedral, in the Chapel of San Biagio, is the most important series of paintings left by Luca Signorelli. In 1504 Signorelli completed the work begun by Beato Angelico in 1447, and painted a magnificent cycle of frescoes which includes the Apocalypse, the Summons of the Elect to Heaven, and the Sentence of the Damned to Hell.

The Cathedral. Detail of the facade and central door. - Many different artists had charge of the construction of the church — among the most noted were Lorenzo Maitani, Andrea and Nino Pisano, Andrea Orcagna and Antonio Federighi — so that the Cathedral of Orvieto can be considered something of a textbook of art history. The facade is enriched by splendid decorations: the bas-reliefs on the base of the composite pillars, created by several different artists, depict stories from the Old Testament, the Gospel and the Last Judgment, while the mosaic in the centre, above the portal — a much restored work by Buccio Leonardelli — represents Our Lady. On 12 August 1970, after a long and bitter controversy, the bronze doors by Emilio Greco were put into place. The artist had been given the commission for the work in 1962 and the doors were cast in 1964; the side doors are of hammered bronze while the central one — seen in the photo — depicts the seven works of mercy.

ANCONA

A colony established by the Dorians in the 4th century B.C., though its history goes back even further, Ancona became one of the most important ports of the Roman Empire, and later the largest city in the Pentapolis, as the colony of the Byzantine Empire here was called. Its history is different from that of the other cities in the region of the Marche, because Ancona has always had to contend with the natural difficulties of its position: a city situated on the sea, but lacking an agriculturally productive hinterland. For this reason during the Middle Ages Ancona inevitably became one of the Italian maritime republics. During its period of maximum expansion, it established commercial outposts in Constantinople, Alexandria, Syria and Rumania. The city itself underwent, as one writer has put it, « the most various influences, Oriental and Slavic, which acted as a centrifugal force, directing outwards the energies of this people, which lives by the sea and for the sea ». The maritime atmosphere can be felt everywhere in Ancona: from the Arch of Trajan, the Basilica of Madonna della Piazza, and the Piazza del Papa, to the Cathedral of San Ciriaco which dominates the city from the heights of the Guasco hill. Not that Ancona is caught up in the past: in fact, it is more flourishing than ever. Its port, naval dockyards, commercial life and industrial developments are the scene of bustling activity, and indicate the extent of Ancona's participation in contemporary affairs.

Santa Maria della Piazza. - The extraordinary harmony and delicacy of the facade, due to the rows of arch motifs and the richly adorned portal in the centre, make this one of the finest churches in the Marche. It was built between 1210 and 1275.

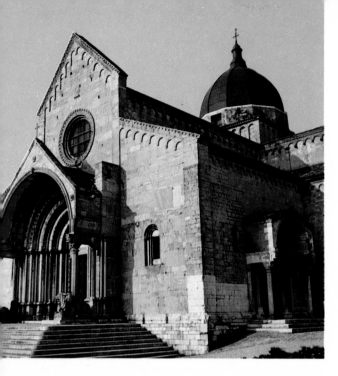

The Cathedral. - The Cathedral of San Ciriaco, standing on the hill of Guasco, dominates the port city of Ancona. Designed in the form of a Greek cross, it was built on the foundations of the Greek temple of Aphrodite Euplea. Dating from the 12th century, its structure is in the Northern Italian style. The fine Gothic portal was added in a later period.

MACERATA. The Cathedral. - Designed by the architect Cosimo Morelli, of Imola, it was built between 1771 and 1790, some time after the town of Macerata had been included in the territory of the Papal States. It stands on the site of a 15th-century church of which the bell-tower remains. The cathedral's facade was never completed.

URBINO. Panorama. - Standing out above the houses of the ancient city is the brick-coloured Palazzo Ducale, built by order of Federico di Monte-feltro and designed by Laurana. It is perhaps the most striking of all the residential palaces built during the Italian Renaissance.

LATIUM

Latium was originally the name of a very small territory situated to the south of the lower Tiber, on the river's left bank, and bounded by the Tyrrhenian Sea, the Latium hills and the slopes of the Tiburtine hills. Almost certainly the name originally meant « level country », and it was closely linked to that of its most ancient inhabitants, the Latins. Historical evidence exists of the formation of a league between its most important cities, dominated by Alba Longa, though this city was later supplanted by Rome, founded, according to historical tradition, on 21 April 753 B.C. With Rome at the head of its league, Latium's long unbroken process of expansion and political unification began, a process almost without historical parallel. The destiny of Latium came to be identified with the destiny of its principal city, Rome, whose achievements have never been equalled in any epoch. No other power in the Eastern or Western worlds has ever succeeded in unifying, under its own laws and language, so many different and distant populations, creating a geographical entity which, besides the Mediterranean basin, included the whole of central and western Europe and even England. Rome first overcame the surrounding tribes, the Volsci and the Equi, subdued the city of Fidenis, destroyed Veius and began to menace the Etruscan territory to the north. As Roman expansion continued, Latium was enlarged until it grew to its present dimensions. It was thus an amalgam of different peoples, and it was only under the emperor Augustus that its administration was organised and unified for the first time. Campania to the south and the two parts of Latium constituted Region I, while the territory north of the Tiber which remained part of Etruria was nominated Region VII. After the fall of the Roman Empire and the conquests of the Byzantines and the Longobards, Latium was reduced in size and began to assume its present-day proportions. But there was agitation for independence in some areas within the region and continual pressure from the invading barbarians from without: against these dispersive tendencies, the Bishop of Rome became an important cohesive force, although the Eastern or Orthodox Church and the Western Catholic Church became increasingly divided. In this early period the Pope's authority was mainly spiritual, although his power was to grow more and more political as time passed. However, the territory of the Papal States did not come into being until the 12th century, and for a long period the aristocratic Roman families of the Colonna, Orsini and Annibaldi vied between themselves for control of the region. Only between the middle of the 14th century and the beginning of the 16th century was papal authority asserted, the barons being repeatedly defeated and the Church's territory unified. Rome and the surrounding region reached one of its periods of maximum splendour during the 16th and 17th centuries, when artists of many different schools and from many countries, invited by the popes, virtually competed with each other to beautify the cities of Latium with their works and monuments. With the beginning of the modern era and the growing ascendancy of secular power, the authority of the popes fell into decline, although the territorial integrity of the Papal States was maintained intact until the end of the 18th century and it was not until the 19th century when it came under Napoleonic domination that the territory began to break up. Later, Latium was divided into two administrative regions, one authority controlling Rome itself and the districts of Tivoli and Subiaco, and the other governing the cities of Velletri, Viterbo, Civitavecchia and Frosinone. In 1870, ten years after the formation of the Kingdom of Italy, Rome was proclaimed capital, and from then on the destiny of Latium was indissolubly linked to that of the capital. Rome came to dominate, from the cultural, political and economic points of view, the smaller cities.

ROME

No other city in the world can be compared with Rome for the vivid sense of the infinite, the universal, the majestic and the grandiose experienced by the visitor. Time here is measured in centuries: centuries of history, civilisation and art. From whatever point of view one sees Rome, it is clear that from its most distant past it has always remained faithful to the aim of its first founders: to create great works that would last through the ages.

At the same time, however, perhaps no other city is so difficult to comprehend as Rome: it has so many different faces, bears the marks of so many different epochs, and contains such an enormous accumulation of artistic and historical treasures. Ancient pagan Rome can be seen in the ruins and great monuments built over a thousand years of civilisation. The revolutionary society of the early Christians, of which so little is known, is present in the catacombs which extend for miles under the city. The majesty of the Renaissance city, which reached the height of its splendour when the power of the popes was at its greatest, links up with the ornamental excesses of the Baroque period. Finally there is modern Rome, capital of an Italy united by the Risorgimento movement of last century, a city continually seeking to maintain a balance between the demands of modernity and the preservation of its ancient heritage. The city of the Seven Hills — though the hills today can hardly be identified, due to changes in the level of the land — was the cradle of a civilisation founded by shepherds, which grew to dominate the then known world. It remained to see the spread of a new religion, and the continuous struggles for power between religious and lay factions, until the final triumph of the Church.

The city's long, complex history has given its inhabitants a particular sort of mentality. The Roman seems blasé and detached, and his philosophy derives from the conviction that « there is nothing he hasn't already seen, and nobody he hasn't already met ». A natural consequence of this philosophy is the ironic or satirical outlook typical of the Romans. But their majestic, vital metropolis, in whose pleasant atmosphere human beings seem more human, justifies as much today as in centuries past its famous title: the Eternal City.

Roman Forum. - Although its title derives from a Latin word meaning open space outside the city, the Forum was actually the heart of the ancient city of Rome. It has been devastated several times by fire, earthquake and the barbarian invasions. During the Middle Ages, its ruins were used as a source of building material; the area was abandoned except for wandering livestock and became familiarly known as the « cow pasture ». The modern excavation projects, which have brought to light so many important archaeological remains, began in the first part of the 19th century on the initiative of the French, and have continued into our own times. In the foreground of the photo can be seen the eight columns and architraves of the pronaos, or colonnaded space in front of the temple of Saturn. Behind them are the ten white columns of the temple of Antoninus and Faustina, within which stands the Baroque facade of San Lorenzo in Miranda, erected in 1602. In the background, standing out against the red mass of the Colosseum, is the church of Santa Francesca Romana.

Roman Forum. - A striking view of this great complex of buildings, centre of the political and administrative life of ancient Rome. The three columns in the foreground are the remains of the temple of Castor and Pollux. Behind them is the Arch of Septimius Severus, built in 203 A.D. to celebrate the military victories of the Emperor and his sons Geta and Caracalla in the eastern part of the Empire.

Colosseum. - This is the most famous monument of ancient Rome. Though commonly called the Colosseum, its more exact name is the Flavian Amphitheatre, because it was begun during the reign of the Flavian emperors. The huge stadium, whose construction took eight years to complete (72-80 A.D.), was used for contests between gladiators and fights against wild beasts. The exact origin of the name « Colosseum » is unknown, though it obviously refers to its vast dimensions. Its plan is in the form of an ellipse, and it has four horizontal sections: three tiers of arcades with Tuscan, Ionic and Corinthian columns, crowned by a series of blind arcades with rectangular windows.

Via dei Fori Imperiali. - This modern « street of the Imperial Forums » links the Colosseum and Piazza Venezia, passing in front of the National Monument. It was built in 1932, and designed to give as complete a view as possible of the grandeur of the ancient forums. On the right is the Roman Forum, and on the left are the Imperial forums.

Colosseum. Interior. - The Colosseum's appearance today is very different from its original splendour: it has been damaged by earthquakes and plundered by medieval builders who used its stones to construct the Palazzo Venezia, the Palazzo della Cancelleria and the river port of Ripetta. Originally it must have been a stupendous sight, dressed with marble, with a huge awning to protect spectators from the sun and rain.

Arch of Constantine. - One of the most majestic monuments of ancient Rome, this arch commemorates the emperor Constantine, famous as the emperor who, in the Edict of Milan in 313, recognised Christianity as the pre-eminent religion of the Roman state. The arch, with its three barrel-vault passageways, was dedicated to Constantine by the Roman Senate in 316 A.D. in honour of his victory over Maxentius.

Campidoglio. - Next to the steep stairway leading up to the 14th-century church of Santa Maria dell'Aracoeli are the more gently sloping steps which climb the Campidoglio Hill. On the top of the hill is the famous Campidoglio Square. Planned by Michelangelo, it contains the Palazzo Senatorio, administrative seat of the municipality of Rome, and the splendid Roman statue of the emperor Marcus Aurelius. On the sides of the stairway are the huge marble statues of the gods Dioscurus, Castor and Pollux.

Castel Sant'Angelo. - Castel Sant'Angelo, among Rome's most important ancient monuments, was begun in 135 A. D. under the emperor Hadrian to serve as his tomb, and the central cylindrical section dates from these works. The emperor Aurelian built its protective walls in 271, and from then on it became a defensive stronghold in continuous use and a safe refuge for the popes during the barbarian invasions and Rome's fierce civil disorders; just as often it served for imprisonment and torture.

St. Peter's. - Regarded by Roman Catholics throughout the world as the centre of their faith, this church stands on the tomb of St. Peter himself. The original basilica of St. Peter's was built by the Emperor Constantine in 326. But in 1452, since it was in a grave state of disrepair, Pope Nicholas V decided to replace it with a completely new building. Many different artists had charge of the project — among them Bernardo Rossellino, Bramante, Raphael, Baldassare Peruzzi and Antonio da Sangallo — but each in turn died before the immense structure could be completed. Finally in 1546, Michelangelo gave the great complex its definitive character, crowning it with his majestic dome.

Via della Conciliazione. - Constructed after the demolition of an old residential area and opened in 1937, this panoramic drive today offers a magnificent view of St. Peter's. The Basilica was consecrated on November 18, 1626, by Pope Urban VIII, after the completion of its imposing facade, designed by the architect Carlo Moderno.

St. Peter's Square. - A view of St. Peter's Square and Via della Conciliazione from Michelangelo's dome, high on the church itself. The square of St. Peter's, a masterpiece of design by the artist Gian Lorenzo Bernini, is one of the most famous sights in the world. The two vast semicircles of its colonnades, which harmonise so well with the irregular shape of the square, were erected between 1656 and 1667 and include no less than 284 columns and 88 pillars. The obelisque in the centre of the square — brought back to Rome from Egypt by the emperor Caligula — was placed here in 1586 by order of Pope Sixtus V; the task involved four months' work by 600 men and 150 horses.

St. Peter's. Interior. - Gian Lorenzo Bernini: *St. Peter's Chair.* The famous chair, one of Bernini's many masterpieces, stands in the apse of St. Peter's. Bernini created a dramatic framework of gilded bronze for the Apostle's throne, which is supported by the huge statues of the Church Fathers, standing more than 16 feet high. Around the throne are luminous clouds, with an angel on either side, and above it is the white dove, symbol of the Holy Spirit.

St. Peter's. Interior. - The huge dimensions of the basilica (it covers a surface area of 165,000 square feet) and the contrast between the richly decorated lateral naves and the relative austerity of the central nave make the interior of St. Peter's an impressive sight. A first glance at the photograph may leave the impression that it is almost of normal size — but a closer examination will reveal that its architecture is of gigantic proportions. In the background of the photo can be seen the canopy which soars above the papal altar. It was designed by Bernini in his most imaginative Baroque style and stands directly under the cupola from which rays of light strike its highly decorated surface.

St. Peter's. Interior. - *Bronze statue of St. Peter.* The statue of the Apostle, seated on a marble throne against the last pillar on the right-hand side of the basilica, was long believed to be a work dating from the 5th century. Indeed, tradition had it that the statue was made from the bronze of the Capitoline Jupiter, melted down by order of Pope Leo I as an act of thanksgiving to the Lord for having granted him the power to appease the barbarian king, Attila the Hun. Modern critics agree, however, that it is much more recent — probably a 13th century work which can perhaps be attributed to Arnolfo di Cambio. This image of the Prince of the Apostles has been greatly venerated for many centuries: in fact, the right foot has been worn away by the kisses of millions of the faithful.

St. Peter's. Interior. - MICHELANGELO BUONARROTI (1475-1564): *Pietà.* This masterpiece by the great Michelangelo, sculpted for the tomb of the French cardinal Jean de Villiers de la Grolaye, abbot of St. Denis, in 1498, is the only work by Michelangelo which carries his signature. It can be seen on the band around the Madonna's left shouder, and there is a tradition which says that Michelangelo engraved his name on the statue one night after hearing an ill-informed guide tell a group of visiting pilgrims from Lombardy that the work was by a Milanese artist. The *Pietà*, sculpted by Michelangelo when he was only 25 years old, is almost disconcerting in the beauty and classical harmony of its lines. The Virgin is depicted as a young woman, calm and resigned to her suffering, and the beautiful body of the Christ is relaxed, not in the rigidity of death but as if in a deep sleep, merely a prelude to his Resurrection.

Sistine Chapel. - Built by order of Pope Sixtus IV between 1475 and 1483 and designed by the Florentine architect Giovanni de Dolci, the Sistine Chapel is famous for its stupendous series of frescoes by Michelangelo, who first painted the huge ceiling (a surface of some 5500 square feet) and later the Last Judgment on the wall behind the altar (2150 square feet). The conclave for the election of the Pope is held here.

Sistine Chapel. - MICHELANGELO BUONARROTI
(1475-1564): *The Creation of Man.* In this
superb fresco, one of nine in the central section
of the Sistine ceiling, Michelangelo depicts God
at the moment when, with a touch of his finger,
he infuses the body of Adam with life. Michelangelo, interested primarily in sculpture, was
convinced against his will by Pope Julius II to
carry out the frescoes of the Sistine ceiling;
having accepted the commission, he spent four
years completing them, from 1508 to 1512. This
was Michelangelo's first major work of fresco
painting and he himself complained that he was
lacking in knowledge of the technique. The
frescoes consist of biblical scenes and the figures of prophets and sibyls. The artist solved the
problem of dividing the enormous surface of
the ceiling by painting on it false architectural
features.

Sistine Chapel. - MICHELANGELO BUONARROTI
(1475-1564): Frescoes of the ceiling: *The Del-
phic Sibyl.* The Sibyl is depicted with a pensive
expression, holding a partly rolled papyrus in
her hand.

Sistine Chapel. - MICHELANGELO BUONARROTI (1475-1564): *The Last Judgment.*
This famous fresco on the end wall of the chapel was commissioned by Pope
Clement VII, and painted by Michelangelo between 1535 and 1541 — twenty-
five years after he had painted the Sistine ceiling. Two windows were walled in
and several frescoes by Perugino and by Michelangelo himself destroyed to make
way for the work. Michelangelo took his inspiration from Dante's « Divine
Comedy » for the central apocalyptic scene of Christ sitting in judgment, with the
elect and the damned on his right and left respectively.

Vatican Museums - *Discobolus* - In a statue of bronze the sculptor Myron, a pupil of Ageladas and Polyclitus (second half of the 5th century B.C.) ventured for the first time to face the problem of representing a moment of maximum effort of the body of an athlete in the act of throwing the discus. When the splendid figure was copied in marble, the unsightly piece of tree trunk was added to keep it balanced and it was signed with the original sculptor's name.

Villa Giulia National Museum - *Sarcophagus of Married Couple*. It comes from Cerveteri and is one of the most interesting records of the high level of Etruscan sculpture in the second half of the 6th century B.C. Husband and wife are reclining on the *kline* in a sitting position, united in death as in life according to Etruscan usage, and are shown in a convivial attitude, tranquilly smiling and dressed in the Etruscan fashion. The woman is wearing a tunic and mantle with the *tutulus* on her head and open-laced footwear. The man's torso is bare and the powerfulness of the frame is skilfully evidenced.

Roman National Museum - *Bronze Statue of a Pugilist*. Greek original of the Hellenistic period, found 1864 in the gardens of Palazzo Colonna (Via 4 Novembre) in Rome. Judging from the position of the figure with the body drawn in and the feet touching, some critics are inclined to place it in the early period of Hellenism (3rd century B.C.) when closed rhythms were still the fashion, while others place it in the last period (1st century B.C.) because it is presented frontwise and lacks the fully-shaped design of the early period.

Vatican Museums - LEONARDO DA VINCI (1452-1519). *St. Jerome*. This work belongs to the artist's first Florentine period or, at the latest, to the beginning of the Milanese one. Even in its unfinished state it is powerfully attractive in the vigour of its design. The preparation of the background and the shading of the models — especially of the saint's head — in this phase of the work allows us to discover his technique as well as to understand his knowledge of anatomy and perspective.

Galleria Borghese - TITIAN [TIZIANO VECELLIO] (1477-1576). *Sacred and Profane Love*. Commonly dated around 1515, *Sacred and Profane Love* is one of the happiest examples of the youthful classicism of Titian. The two mysterious female figures, monumental and alive as Greek statues, merge into the countryside at sunset and are bathed in the same colourful light.

193

Basilica of Santa Maria Maggiore. - The church's main facade, a splendid work by the Florentine architect Ferdinando Fuga erected between 1743 and 1750, has two structures of equal size on either side and stands on the square of Santa Maria Maggiore. The Romanesque bell-tower, the highest in Rome, is matched by the column taken from the ancient Roman Basilica of Maxentius, which was brought here in 1614 and on which was placed a bronze statue of the Madonna.

Basilica of Santa Maria Maggiore. Interior. - The church was begun in 431 by order of Pope Sixtus III, and the interior retains its original primitive appearance, even though many new elements have been added over the centuries. Among these are the floor, put down in the 12th century, and the richly decorated wooden ceiling, attributed to Giuliano da Sangallo and erected in the 16th century. The canopy with its red porphyry columns over the main altar was designed by Fuga in the 18th century.

Basilica of St. John Lateran and Gate of St. John. A fine view of the square and church of St. John Lateran, seat of the Bishop of Rome. Like so many others, the church has been considerably altered and its present-day appearance is the 17th century version designed by the architect Borromini, commissioned for the work by Pope Innocent X. On top of the facade, designed by Alessandro Galilei in 1735, is a series of fourteen statues of the Apostles and Saints, with the statue of Christ the Redeemer standing above them. In the foreground can be seen the city gate of San Giovanni, built in the Aurelian Wall in 1574 by order of Pope Gregory XIII. The gate stands at the beginning of the Via Appia Nuova.

Basilica of St. Paul-without-the-walls. - Built last century by the architects Belli, Bosio, Camporese and Paoletti, it stands on the place where the Apostle Paul was buried after his martyrdom between 64 and 68 A.D. The several churches built on the same site in preceding epochs were destroyed by various misfortunes, or because, as its name states, the church was outside the city walls and thus particularly vulnerable to the depredations of invading armies. In the photo can be seen the facade with its mosaics, created by Francesco Vespignami to designs by Filippo Agricola and Nicola Consoni. In the foreground, at the centre of the cloister, is the fine statue of St. Paul by Giuseppe Obici.

Trinità dei Monti. - Another picturesque view of Rome, this time from the Piazza di Spagna. In the foreground is the fountain called the « Barcaccia », by the Florentine Pietro Bernini, father of the famous Baroque artist Gian Lorenzo Bernini. Behind it are the « Spanish Steps », a stairway of travertine stone designed by Alessandro Specchi and Francesco De Sanctis (1723-26). Above is the square of Trinità dei Monti, with its obelisque brought here from the Sallustian Gardens, and the church of the same name, begun in 1502 by will of King Louis XII of France, and restored in the 19th century by Francesco Mazois.

St. Peter-in-Chains. - According to tradition, Eudoxia, wife of the emperor Valentinian III, wanted a church built in which to preserve the chains (« vincula » in Latin) with which St. Peter was bound during his imprisonment at Jerusalem and Rome. From this tradition derives the name of San Pietro in Vincoli, which was consecrated by Pope Sixtus III in 439. It was much restored and modified during the Renaissance period under Pope Julius II, and again in the 18th century by Francesco Fontana. The Renaissance facade with five arches resting on octagonal pillars was previously attributed to Baccio Pontelli, but modern critics tend to believe it is the work of Meo di Caprino.

St. Peter-in-Chains. Interior. - MICHELANGELO BUONARROTI (1475-1564): *Moses.* Sculpted for the tomb of Pope Julius II, this is the only statue completed of the many planned in Michelangelo's grandiose original conception of the tomb. But Michelangelo's powerful genius is fully expressed in the statue of Moses: the great Hebrew law-maker is depicted full of scorn and anger for the idolators among his people, and a combination of human and almost divine feeling emerges from its dramatic tension. The masterpiece can also be interpreted as a reflection of the state of mind, character, and deepest feelings of the artist himself.

St. Peter-in-Chains. Interior. - The spacious interior is divided into three naves by twenty fluted marble columns, splendid examples with Doric capitals and Ionic bases. The wooden ceiling, of shallow vault design, frames the fresco by G.B. Parodi, « The Miracle of the Chains ». In the circular apse, with its frescoes by Giacomo Coppi painted in 1577, is the high altar, covered by a canopy designed by Virgilio Vespignani, and containing the urn in which St. Peter's chains are kept.

Fountain of Trevi. - The fountain was designed by the Roman architect Nicolò Salvi by order of the Florentine Pope, Clement XII, to give a worthy outlet to the waters of the « Virgin Spring » (Acqua Vergine), so called because of the ancient tradition that a maiden had shown its whereabouts to thirsty Roman soldiers. In 19 B.C. Agrippa had the water source linked to his baths in Rome by means of an aqueduct more than twelve miles long. When Salvi designed the fountain, he placed it against one wall of the palace of the Poli dukes, combining this architectural framework with statues representing mythological figures by the Roman sculptore Pietro Bracci. The fountain was completed in 1762, and was called the Fountain of Trevi because of its position at a « Treio » or « trivio », that is the meeting point of three streets. This is the fountain into which visitors to Rome, both Italians and foreigners, throw a coin: according to the tradition, this act will ensure their return to the Eternal City.

Piazza Navona. - The finest of the squares created in Rome during the Baroque period, Piazza Navona repeats the outlines of the Roman stadium of Domitian. In the foreground is the Fontana del Moro (Fountain of the Moor), while in the centre of the square is Bernini's famous Fountain of the Rivers. On the left is the church of Sant'Agnese in Agone, designed by Francesco Borromini.

The Duomo. - The cathedral, dedicated to San Lorenzo, is of Romanesque design, though it had already been much altered by unfortunate restorations before the addition of the insipid facade in the middle of the 16th century. Worth noting, however, are the windows of the original church and the splendid Romanesque rose-window on the right-hand side. The original Romanesque church was probably built around 1190, when a group of Longobard architects became active in the city. The fine bell-tower standing on the left-hand side of the cathedral was remodelled during the 14th century, and the upper part completely transformed by the addition of decorative motives in travertine and peperino stone, along with its mullioned windows and octagonal spire.

Palazzo dei Papi. - Beside the cathedral stands Viterbo's most important building from a historical point of view: the battlemented Palace of the Popes. Built between 1255 and 1266 when the popes often resided in Viterbo (several sensational conclaves were held here), it saw the most important events in the city's history during the Middle Ages, events always involving one of the various popes. The elegant loggia supported by its large arch and the stairway leading up to the palace contribute to the building's majesty and grace.

ABRUZZO AND MOLISE

The region of Abruzzi and Molise first comes to historical notice in the first half of the 5th century B.C. with the Samnites, a mainly mountain-dwelling people who lived in the inaccessible zones of Molise and Matese, their most important cities being Isernia, Boiano and Venafro. Towards 470 B.C. the Samnites began a campaign of progressive expansion south-west into Campania, and this was the principal factor which led to the degeneration of their civilisation, because the territories they conquered in Campania formed a confederation which detached itself from the Samnites' mountainous home region, leaving it isolated and weakened. Soon afterwards the Samnites had their first contact with the Romans and this led almost immediately to war. The first Roman colonies were founded: Amiterno, Alba and Teate. Rebellions against Roman rule when they took place were bloodily repressed, and finally Silla wiped what had been the Samnite nation from the Italian map. The early Christians formed their first dioceses in what was left of the principal cities: Amiterno and Sulmona became the first episcopal seats. The conquest by the Franks of the northern part of the Abruzzi led only to a further weakening of the region, which also suffered at the hands of the Saracen raiders. Then in the middle of the 11th century the Normans, advancing towards the hinterland, overcame the defenders and within a few short years had control of the whole region, introducing their feudal and military society. Of great importance for the Abruzzi was the king Charles of Anjou, who must be considered the real founder of the city of Aquila. For almost two and a half centuries, this city assumed such a leading role in the region that its destiny and that of the city became indistinguishable. The main achievement of the Aragonese rulers who succeeded the Angevins was the imposing of a measure of order on the seasonal pastoral industry, which for centuries had been the main source of production for the Abruzzi people. The history of the region during the 16th century, under Spanish domination, has no particular features worthy of note. In the middle of the 17th century there was a republican rebellion, with anti-feudal objectives, allied with the uprising led by Masaniello in Naples, though in Aquila it had markedly autonomous features. There was an exceptional and unexpected reawakening in the second half of the 18th century when men like Cuoco, Zurlo and Galanti brought in the Bourbon reforms, showing considerable wisdom and a finally clear consciousness of the political and historical situation of the region. However, after the Bourbon restoration, public works were deplorably neglected, and the rebellious movements which broke out in parts of the region were harshly repressed. As in all the regions of southern Italy, the most important social phenomena in Abruzzo-Molise are the pastoral industry, banditry and emigration, all three of which are causally linked. Unfortunately these unhappy facts of life have given birth to a sort of literature which has distorted their real significance, giving them a false romantic and idyllic colouring which conceals their dramatic reality. As a step towards solving the grave problems of this fertile zone the Government, in its recent decision to create administratively autonomous regions in Italy, divided Abruzzi and Molise into two distinct regions; at the same time a second province was created in Molise, and Isernia was chosen as its capital city.

L'AQUILA

Aquila stands in the valley of the Aterno River, on a hill which slopes gently down towards the plain; it therefore commands an excellent strategic position, further fortified by the sturdy walls surrounding the city. Aquila is known as « the city of ninety-nine ». Its annals relate that the city was born from the union of ninety-nine castles. Around the ninety-nine castles were built ninety-nine churches, ninety-nine squares and ninety-nine fountains. Today the ravages of time have greatly reduced the number of these monuments, but there is still the fountain called the Fontana della Riviera which has ninety-nine outlets, and from the Torre Palazzo tower nearby the ninety-nine peals of its bell ring out. Aquila's period of greatest splendour began in the year 1294 when Pope Celestine V was invested in the Basilica of Santa Maria in Collemaggio in the presence of Charles II of Anjou, and in the following years many fine buildings were constructed. Its architecture shows the influence of many different schools, among them those of Apulia, Rome and Lombardy, but one can distinguish an original and fundamentally Romano-Gothic style which was to last until the middle of the 15th century.

Unfortunately the zone in which Aquila is built is extremely prone to earthquakes, and this fact has caused its progressive deterioration.

Aquila today has still very much the atmosphere of a busy medieval town, with its circle of walls, its long, narrow streets, and the picturesque facades of its churches. Life in the older areas has a rhythm very much as it could have been centuries ago, slower and more tranquil, seeming to ignore the implacable progress which is transforming the more modern areas of the city.

Santa Maria in Collemaggio. - Begun in 1287 by Pietro Angeleri da Morrone, who was to become Pope Celestine V, the church is a splendidly original example of Romanesque architecture, noteworthy for the effect created by the contrast of red and white stone on its facade. The octagonal tower which stands out from the building on the right-hand side of the facade originally supported a bell-tower, demolished in 1545. The church contains the remains of Pope Celestine V, who died in prison at Fumone in 1296, after having abdicated the papal throne.

TERAMO. The Cathedral. - Begun in the 12th century by the count-bishop Guido, it has been reconstructed several times, so that of the original building all that remains is the fine central portal. The portal, a work by Deodato dei Cosmati, consists of a Roman arch surmounted by a tall pointed gable of Gothic inspiration. The bell-tower on the right of the church is Romanesque in style and has an octagonal bell-chamber surmounted by a spire. It was built in 1483 and is similar to many others to be seen in the region.

CHIETI. The Duomo. - Although the Cathedral of San Giustino is very old, it has unfortunately been considerably altered over the centuries. The first modifications were carried out in the year 840; in 1592 it was almost completely rebuilt, and it was further impaired by restoration works in 1770 and in 1877. The fine bell-tower, reminiscent of the tower on the Cathedral of Atri, was begun in 1335 but not completed until 163 years later. The tower originally had a spire at the summit, but it was destroyed by an earthquake in 1706, and has never been entirely rebuilt.

CAMPANIA

In early times, the prehistoric inhabitants of Campania came into contact with the Greeks: at the beginning of the historical era Greek navigators began colonising the region. Towards the middle of the 8th century B.C., they founded first the city of Cumae, and later Pozzuoli and Naples. By the middle of the 6th century, the Etruscans had penetrated into the region from the north, but they did not succeed in entirely displacing the

Greek settlers. Instead, they merged with them, assimilating the most important elements of their way of life, thus creating a juxtaposition of two different cultures rather than a new civilisation. The Etruscans themselves were displaced in the second half of the 5th century B.C. by the Samnites, whose dominion extended as far as Cumae and Capua. At the same time, the power of Rome was growing, and the Romans began their gradual infiltration of Campania in the 4th century B.C., gaining complete control of the region in little more than half a century. During the first centuries of the Roman Empire, Campania was the preferred residence of many nobles and emperors. After the fall of the Roman Empire, the integrity of the region began to break up in the face of the frequent barbarian invasions during the 5th century, Alaric attacking it from the north and Genseric from the south. In the early Middle Ages, however, two of Campania's cities, Naples and Amalfi, were the most important and powerful cities in the whole of Italy. In 1030, the Norman military leader Rainolf Drengot was named Count of Aversa by King Sergio IV of Naples because of his assistance against the Longobard king, Pandolfo IV of Capua. This was the first step in the Norman conquest of Campania. Only forty-seven years later, Robert the Guiscard was to attack Naples from Salerno. The Normans had fluctuating fortunes in their battles against the Neapolitans up until 1139, but when Ruggero II entered Naples a Norman kingdom had already been set up, uniting most of southern Italy. The capital of the kingdom remained Palermo, in Sicily, though the Neapolitans refused to take second place to the Sicilian city. Under the Swabian dynasty, Naples became the kingdom's cultural capital, and in 1224 the emperor Frederick II founded its university. On his death, the people invited Charles of Anjou to govern them, and in 1266 this king finally transferred the capital from Palermo to Naples. The Angevins ruled until the 15th century; in 1442 they were replaced by the Aragonese dynasty, supported by the people, and Charles VIII arrived in Naples in 1494. Campania became a battlefield once more during the Franco-Spanish wars for possession of southern Italy, until on 1 January 1504, with the fall of the fortress of Gaeta, the kingdom's independence came to an end. The Neapolitan people led many attempted insurrections against their Spanish rulers, but all of them were put down. The revolt against the government in June 1647 brought the figure of Masaniello into the limelight, but once more the Spaniards had little difficulty in restoring order. The struggles against foreign rulers continued during the following period of rule by the Bourbon dynasty, which lasted from 1734 until 1860. In 1798 there was the brief respite of the short-lived Parthenopean Republic, supported by the French, but when Napoleon's progress suffered a setback Naples was regained by the Bourbons, who fled again when Napoleon's brother Josef reconquered the city. After the final downfall of the French emperor, the Bourbons returned to the throne of Naples and began filling its prisons with the patriots who had dreamt of liberty. Bourbon rule came to an end on 7 September 1860, when Garibaldi entered the city of Naples. With the unification of Italy, solutions were sought to all the problems which had been created or put aside during the many centuries of domination by foreign rulers, first of all the problem of banditry, and more recently that of large-scale emigration.

NAPLES

The famous travellers of past eras never failed to make Naples one of their stopping-places. They were drawn there by the knowledge that they would find a city and a people strangely unique. Even in the Europe of today, reduced by the equalising power of progress, Naples remains without parallel, a sort of « nation within a nation ». Its own peculiar traditions and customs are accentuated by their contrast with the modern way of life, which here, for a long and complicated series of reasons, has never led to that complete substitution of the old for the new to be seen elsewhere. The vitality of Naples stems from the extroverted nature of its people: the Neapolitans always behave as if they were in their own home, in public or in private, consuming vast quantities of energy in a histrionic display which sometimes seems to have no more point than a gesture made simply for the pleasure of making it. This apparently self-destructive behaviour is in reality a

way of maintaining a sort of dignity and of not succumbing to adversity.

Proverbially the city of light and sun, Naples has innumerable narrow streets and dark alleys. Its people, almost idolatrous in their religious faith, are at the same time capable of remarkable irreverence. Such contrasts can be understood when one sees the city itself: its monuments and institutions, no matter how mighty, have never dominated its sense of life.

Founded by farmers from Cumae in the 2nd century B.C., Naples has seen many rulers: from the Romans to the Byzantine emperors, from the Norman and Swabian kings to the Angevin and Aragonese monarchs. But it was perhaps the domination by the Spanish Crown, into whose hands the city fell in 1503, which had the greatest impact on its history. Not until the accession of the Bourbon dynasty in 1734, when it became the capital of an independent kingdom, did Naples return to its former splendour.

Angevin pier. - The origins of this port area, which is in front of Piazza del Municipio, are thought to go back to the time of Charles II of Anjou, that is to the beginning of the 14th century. In the foreground of the photograph is the new passenger terminal from which travellers leave for innumerable destinations: in fact Naples, though second to Genoa in cargo shipments, is the biggest passenger port in Italy.

Piazza Municipio. - This square is the commercial and economic centre of Naples, and offices of all sorts are housed in the buildings which surround it. Previously it was planted, throughout its entire length and breadth, with holm-oaks, whose shade allowed the passer-by to cross the square sheltered from the sun. It was reluctantly decided to remove these magnificent trees so as to make more room for traffic.

Castel Nuovo. - The Castel Nuovo, or « New Castle », was so called from the date of its construction so as to distinguish it from pre-existing castles, though it is also commonly known as the Maschio Angioino, or « Angevin Keep », because it was built by Charles I of Anjou between 1279 and 1282. Modified by Alfonso of Aragon in the middle of the 15th century, it became the focal point of the struggles for power between the various royal houses who ruled the kingdom. Among the castle's famous guests were Pope Celestine V, Giotto, who was summoned by King Robert to paint the frescoes in the Palatine Chapel, and Petrarch, who stayed here before going on to Rome to be crowned Poet Laureate in the Campidoglio. Boccaccio was never a guest in the castle, but it was he who described the brilliant chivalrous circle which gravitated around the Angevin court. The towers on the main facade also have names: that on the left is called the « Torre di San Giorgio », the central one the « Torre di Mezzo », and the right-hand one the « Torre della Guardia ». Between these last two, as can be seen in the photograph, is the Renaissance arch of triumph, probably designed by Luciano Laurana (1420-c. 1480). The imposing Castel Nuovo gives a clear idea of the impressive grandeur of a medieval castle.

Porta Capuana. - Built in 1484 and designed by Giuliano da Maiano, this is one of the finest and best-preserved of Naples' Renaissance city gates. Its construction was the result of the decision by Ferdinand I of Aragon to rebuild and extend the ancient city walls. Between the two towers, called the Towers of Honour and of Virtue, is the elegant archway which stands in graceful contrast with the otherwise massive dimensions of the structure.

Piazza Sannazzaro. - A view by night of the fountain in this square, which is named after the great humanist and philosopher, Jacopo Sannazzaro. Sannazzaro lived here for many years after Frederick of Aragon granted him in 1497 a huge area of land called « Mergelino », later to become one of the most famous parts of Naples, the present-day « Mergellina ».

Gallery of Humbert I. - Built between the years 1887 and 1890 and designed by the architect Emanuele Rocca, it is one of the very rare examples in Naples of the « iron architecture » which had such an important place in architectural developments at the end of last century. It was constructed as one of the many rebuilding projects which have, little by little, so greatly changed the appearance of Naples. Today the gallery remains in some respects the heart of Neapolitan life — partly because, designed in the form of a cross, it connects streets and squares which are among the most important in the city's history, and partly because it has been for many years the theatrical centre of Naples. The modern lyricists who carry on the tradition of the Neapolitan song meet here.

Royal Palace. - It was built by Domenico Fontana between 1600 and 1602. The unusual appearance of its facade is due to an error in calculation on the part of the designer: in fact, in the middle of the 18th century, several cracks appeared which were thought to be the result of structural deterioration, and as a result, on the advice of Luigi Vanvitelli, every second arch was bricked in. The equestrian statue standing on the left is by Antonio Canova, and represents the Bourbon king, Charles III.

Royal Palace. Main staircase. - This monumental staircase, designed by Francesco Picchiatti and built in 1750, leads up to the royal apartments on the first floor. The stairs, constructed in delicate shades of marble, are adorned by works of sculpture by Gennaro di Crescenzo, Tito Angelini and Angelo Solari.

Church of San Francesco da Paola. - On one side of the spacious Piazza Plebiscito is the vast arc of the colonnade belonging to the church of San Francesco da Paola. Ferdinand I had the church built in 1826 as a votive offering after he had regained his kingdom. It was incorporated with the colonnade, which was already standing, and an attempt was clearly made — though only partially successful — to reproduce the simple lines of the Roman Pantheon.

Panorama of Naples from the Charterhouse of San Martino. - From the balcony looking over the gulf, the visitor has an unparalleled view of the sprawling shell-shaped city beneath.

Palace of Capodimonte. - The palace was built in the middle of a magnificent park for the Bourbon king Charles III, who commissioned its design from Giovanni Antonio Medrano in 1739. The king, a « hunter of furred and feathered beasts in the sight of God » as he liked to describe himself, had planned to construct a simple hunting lodge, but changed his mind when he decided to house here the art collections inherited from his mother Elisabetta Farnese. The beautiful park, with its profusion of tall trees, mainly pines, holm-oaks and palms, is laid out according to the design of the German architect Dehnhardt. In it, apart from the palace, are the Chapel of San Gennaro and the well-known factory which up until 1805 produced the famous Capodimonte porcelain, sought by collectors throughout the world.

National Museum. - TITIAN (1490-1576): *Pope Paul III Farnese with his nephews.*

National Museum. - MASACCIO (1401-1428): *Crucifixion.*

Palace of Capodimonte. One of the halls. - The photograph conveys something of the size and splendour of the rooms of the palace, and gives an idea of the money spent to embellish it. Today the palace houses one of the most important art collections in Europe. The gallery is organised along extremely logical lines, and has modern facilities which include, apart from its air-conditioning plant, a complex system of mobile lighting which permits perfect illumination of the works exhibited at all hours of the day.

National Museum. - *Eros punished by Venus*. This fresco is among the many found in the buildings of the ancient cities excavated from beneath the lava of Vesuvius. The works are usually by humble artists, but they have a considerable importance for the understanding of the customs of the people.

National Museum. - *Paquius Proculus and his wife*. A fresco discovered in a house in Pompeii.

National Museum. - *Venus and Mars*. A fresco which comes from Pompeii and can be dated around the beginning of the 1st century.

National Museum. - *The Battle of Issus.*
This magnificent mosaic, which depicts
the battle between Alexander the
Great and Darius, was discovered in
Pompeii in the House of Faunus. Of
great artistic merit, it represents the decisive moment in the battle, when the
army of Alexander gains the upper hand.
In the photo is Darius, standing in his
chariot and apparently urging on his
troops to a final effort: dismay can be
seen in the eyes of the general as he
realises that defeat is now inevitable.

National Museum. - *Sea creatures,* mosaic.
This mosaic was part of the floor uncovered in the House of the Faun.

POMPEII

« I know of nothing more interesting », Goethe said of Pompeii. And indeed here, as a result of a natural disaster, an entire Roman city has been maintained intact in all the aspects of its daily life. Pompeii does not contain the ruins of a city abandoned only after a long decline. The rain of lava from Vesuvius put a sudden halt to all its normal activities, and innumerable stories can thus be reconstructed from the discoveries made during its excavation.

Pompeii was founded in the 8th century B.C., on the Tyrrhenian coast, to serve as a port for important cities such as Nola, Nocera and Acerra. It was ruled first by Greeks from Cumae, and later by the Samnite people. It was during the long rule of the Samnites that the city was given the basic appearance which can be seen today, the surrounding walls, the arena, the theatre, the temple of Jupiter and the Stabian baths. In 80 B.C. Pompeii became a Roman colony, opening a new phase in its development, during which the temples of Venus, of Isis and of the Concordia Augusta, besides the new baths, were

constructed, and the Forum rebuilt. The fifteen thousand inhabitants were thus immersed in their busy, peaceful life, and were recovering from the disastrous damage caused by an earthquake in 62 A.D., when on the 24th of August, 79, at a little after midday, a dark cloud rose with a great roar from Vesuvius, blacking out the sky. A light shower of ashes began to fall, followed immediately by bigger and bigger fragments of rock. Suffocating sulphur fumes poured down from the mountain penetrating into all its houses. Forty-eight hours later, the sun was shining again, but the city had disappeared, and no less than one thousand six hundred years passed before Domenico Fontana, during canal works, discovered by chance some remains. Only under Charles II of Bourbon in 1748 were official excavations begun, after it had been ascertained from inscriptions uncovered that the remains were those of the ancient city of Pompeii. After the unification of Italy in the 19th century, the excavations were put on a scientific basis, and have thus led to the rediscovery of 60 per cent of the city.

Porta Marina. - This was the gate which gave access to Pompeii on the western side, and it is the entranceway normally used today. The gate's name in ancient times is uncertain: it may have had the name still used today, or it may have been called « Porta Portuensis », due to the fact that a road leads from here to the port, linking it with the city. The two passageways which can be seen were used by pedestrians and mule-drivers respectively; the steep incline prevented the gate's being used by vehicles.

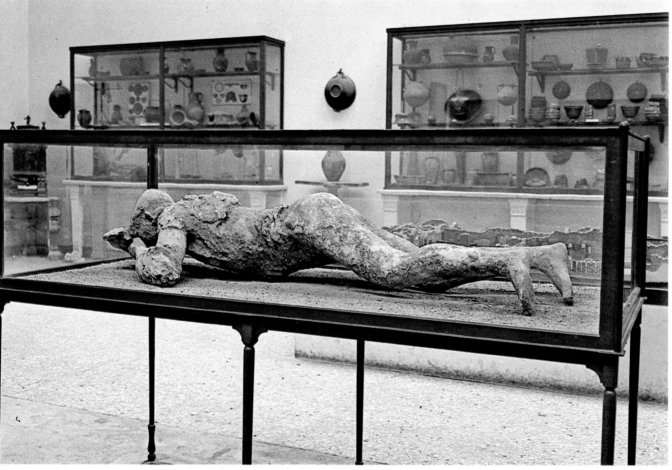

Antiquarium. - In these rooms are exhibited objects of great interest from which it is possible to reconstruct something of the domestic environment and the final tragedy of Pompeii. The illustrations show some of the most impressive casts from the collection. The technique by which the casts were obtained was used for the first time by Fioravanti, who poured plaster into the cavities left by human bodies or other organisms which had decomposed in the solidified volcanic ashes. Above left is reproduced the *Watch-dog from the House of Orpheus.* The dog was forgotten in the general confusion of the flight from the lava, and left tied to the entrance of the house; for as long as the length of its chain permitted, the dog was able to breath by staying above the mounting layer of ash, but when this was no longer possible it was suffocated trying to break the chain with its teeth. Below left is the cast of the *Body of a Young Woman,* lying face downwards with the right hand supporting the head and the body partly stripped of the clothing which covered it. Above right is a cast of the *Crouching Mule-driver,* found against the walls of the Grande Palestra in the vain attempt to escape; the unhappy man tried to save himself from the deadly swirling ashes by covering himself with his cloak.

Antiquarium. - *Statue of Ephebe (Young Man).* - This statue, which is basically an imitation of classical Greek models from the 5th century B.C., was found in the house of Marcus Fabius Rufus, who came from Rome with Pompeii's conquerors and was thus related to the famous dictator, Fabius Maximus the Cunctator. The statue, like others found in Pompeii such as the Lychnophoros Ephebe, had been used as a fruit-stand, a practice fairly common in the more ostentatious homes of the rich, as Lucretius relates in his *De Rerum Natura* (11, 24).

Temple of Apollo. - Built at the height of the Samnite era in about the 3rd century B.C. on a site which was already sacred ground, the temple has a portico with 48 columns converted into the Corinthian style during restorations carried out in the age of Nero; the fluting on the lower part of the columns has been filled in to avoid their deterioration. The walls are painted with scenes from the *Iliad* popular at the time, such as the anger of Achilles and the death of Hector. Numerous statues stood in the area where the religious rites took place.

The basilicas. - The basilicas of Pompeii, like those in all the Roman cities, were public buildings, mostly situated in the vicinity of the forum, and used for various purposes connected with the city's public life: some of them contained courts of law, some were used for commercial transactions or political meetings, and others were frequented by leisurely passers-by who stopped there to stroll or chat with friends, much as Europeans do in their present-day cafés. The basilica of Pompeii, the city's most important public building, has a majestic entrance facing towards the forum with a spacious vestibule. The interior is divided into naves by slender Corinthian columns, and at the end on a raised platform is the judges' tribunal. Under the tribunal, below ground level, is a cell which may have been used to hold convicted prisoners awaiting sentence.

Western portico of the forum. - Transformation of the older, more modest forum built by the Samnites was begun by the Romans not long after their conquest of the city, but they retained the outlines and the alignment from north to south of the original area. The forum was closed to vehicles and beasts of burden, and thus reserved for pedestrians, the real leaders in the public life of Italic and Roman cities. The basic significance of the « Forum » in Italic, and consequently Roman, town-planning is well known: a concept still valid today, it consisted of a small area at the centre of the city, around which were grouped all the buildings which, as seats of government bodies or of other public institutions, formed the fulcrum of the city's political, religious and economic life. Unfortunately the Romans' plans to renovate the forum of Pompeii were never fully realised. They were temporarily interrupted by the earthquake in 62 A. D., and then halted, this time permanently, by the eruption of Vesuvius in 79.

Casa del Fauno. - The house takes its name from the fact that a fine bronze figure depicting the Roman pastoral god Faunus was found in its impluvium during the course of excavations. The original has since been transferred to the Archeological Museum in Naples, but a copy can still be seen standing where it was first discovered. The House of Faunus is one of the largest and richest dwellings known from the Samnite era (2nd century B. C.), though all its architectural elements are at least partly derived from Greek or Italian influences.

Millwheels on the Via Consolare. - The period of internal strife which caused a reduction in wealth throughout the city forced many middle-class families to take up commercial activities by converting parts of their dwellings into stores or workshops. In this house, for instance, the family kept one section as living quarters, but converted the garden into a mill for making bread, with millwheels turned either by manpower or by animals.

Casa dei Vetti. Colonnade. - This house seems to have belonged to two merchants, probably brothers, whose considerable success in business apparently allowed them to construct a dwelling luxurious enough to conceal their modest social origins. In fact, the House of the Vetti is one of the most important of the Roman residential buildings in Pompeii inhabited by its wealthiest citizens. Apart from the exemplary arrangement of its living quarters, the house is justly famous for its rich wall decorations, which belong to Pompeii's so-called « fourth style ». The excavation works at Pompeii have been carried out with extreme care and originality: each area uncovered has been left as it was, so as to give the visitor a vivid idea of the day-to-day life of the city. The insight into this life given by the residential and public areas, thus restored to their original layout, makes an unforgettable impression.

ISCHIA PONTE - Ischia and Capri, the two magnificent islands in the Gulf of Naples, are so well known that describing them is hardly necessary. Ischia, the green island, famous for its pine forests, thermal springs, and vineyards, which produce a rare and exquisite wine, is the largest in the archipelago (about 18 square miles) and has several towns. At Ischia Ponte, situated at the end of the inhabited area, is the Aragonese bridge, so called because Alfonso of Aragon had it built in 1438 to link the small island on which the castle is built to the island of Ischia itself.

CAPRI. The Faraglioni rocks. - Capri's geographical position and climatic conditions, with its perennial flowers and rugged, picturesque coastline, make it one of the most beautiful islands in the world. Geologists say that Capri is not of volcanic origin, but rather formed from dolomitic limestone. The island's coast, with its many grottos, is lined with sheer cliffs and fantastically shaped rocks which seem almost to defend it from the sea. Among the best-known of these strange rock formations are the Faraglioni, so well-known in fact — even to people who have never been to Capri, but have seen photographs of it — that there is no need to describe them.

APULIA

PUGLIA

ISOLE TREMITI

ABRUZZO E MOLISE

a TERMOLI

Rodi di Gargano

Apricena

Vieste

M.CALVO 1056

Manfredonia

Golfo di Manfredonia

Lucera

FOGGIA

M.CORNACCHIA 1151

Ortonova

Margherita di S.

Barletta

Trani

a BENEVENTO

Cerignola

Bovino

Canosa di P.

Morfetta

BARI

ANCONA VENEZIA

Mare Adriatico

PORTI DEL LEVANTE

a NAPOLI

Minervino

Bitonto

Mola di Bari

Monópoli

CAMPANIA

Altamura

Alberobello

Monticelli

a POTENZA

Ostuni

BRINDISI

Castellaneta

Grottaglie

Mesagne

BASILICATA

TARANTO

Manduria

LECCE

a CROTONE

Galatone

Otranto

Gallipoli

Màglie

Mare Tirreno

Golfo di Taranto

CROTONE REGGIO C.

S.Maria di Leuca

CATANIA MALTA

CALABRIA

mont.

In the year 706 B.C. Spartan colonists from Laconia (legend has it that they were guided by Phalantos) founded at the northernmost point of the eastern Ionic coast the city of Taras, which four centuries later was to become Taranto. Its ideal geographical position was the main reason why, in a brief space of time, Taranto was able to impose its political authority on the other peoples in the region, and this was the period of greatest splendour in the city's history. However, as its economic and cultural riches grew, the Spartan virtues of its founders diminished, and thus Taranto came to entrust its defence to mercenary soldiers. In 326 B.C. Rome had already cast its eyes on the powerful Apulian city. The « Pyrrhic victories » made famous by Pyrrhus, the King the Tarantines had called to their aid from Epirus, were not convincing enough, and after their first defeat near Benevento in 275 they were finally overcome by the Romans in 272 B.C. The task of Romanising Apulia was interrupted by Rome's war with Carthage, but when the latter finally collapsed at Zama, Rome's colonisation of Apulia was resumed. Taranto fell into increasingly rapid decline, though the prosperity of Brindisi grew with equal rapidity, because it was from this port that the Roman legions set sail for the East. Apulia had a flourishing economy and culture under Augustus and during the first two centuries of the Roman Empire, when its commercial contacts wtih Egypt, Greece and Syria transformed it into a gateway to the Orient. In the 3rd century Christianity reached the region. In the following period, after the fall of the Roman Empire, Apulia suffered a series of invasions. First it was conquered by the Byzantines whose harsh taxation system bore heavily on its already distressed inhabitants; then in 590 the Longobards arrived, to be succeeded in the first half of the 9th century by the Muslims, who attacked, occupied and sacked Brindisi and Taranto. In 880, during the revival of the Byzantine Empire's power, Apulia passed once more under its control. It became the scene of the interminable struggles between the Byzantine Empire and the Germanic Holy Roman Empire, and there was also discord of a religious sort. From the year 1000 rebellious movements against the Byzantine rulers intensified, and the Normans ably took advantage of them, so that in 1043 the Norman leader William of Hauteville became Count of Apulia. Under the Normans and later under the Swabian dynasty, Apulia entered into a period of prosperity, in which its trading ties with distant lands increased and its art and culture flourished, especially under the emperor Frederick II of Swabia who made the region his favourite residence. When the House of Swabia died out, the domination of the Angevin dynasty began, and Charles I of Apulia surrendered the region with little resistance. In 1442 rule over Apulia passed to the Aragonese, who neglected it in favour of Spain itself. The total abandon into which it fell continued for the two centuries during which it was governed by the Spaniards, whose commercial interests all lay in the Atlantic and thus excluded Apulia from its previously important role. In 1707 it was occupied by the Austrians though they retained control only until 1738 when the treaty of Vienna assigned the entire kingdom of Naples to Charles of Bourbon. Later, during the decade of French domination, important reforms were realised, until with the collapse of the Napoleonic Empire the kingdom was regained by Ferdinand IV of Bourbon who became Ferdinand I, king of the Two Sicilies. Only with Italy's unification in 1861 did Apulia see an end to its eternal wars and foreign rulers.

BARI

On April 25, 1813, when Gioacchino Murat — installed by Napoleon as King of Naples in 1808 — signed the decrees authorising the city's development, a turning point was reached in the history of Bari. Previously, closed within the circle of its old city walls, Bari had been a well-known centre, but no more important than many others in the region of Apulia. Then began the rapid process of economic and cultural growth which was to make it the leading city on the Adriatic coast of southern Italy. Historically, Bari goes back to Roman times, but after Roman domination it had a variety of rulers, first the Byzantines, then the Saracens, then the Byzantines once more, until it came under the rule of the Neapolitan regime, continuing in this modest existence until the 18th century. The city is built on the coast and surrounded by the warm colours of the Adriatic Sea. Its people, noted for their tenaciousness, speak a strange dialect which is a mixture of the most diverse languages. And its economic and cultural activities are not limited to Italy itself: it has a constant interest in the Near East countries facing it across the Adriatic, for whom its annual Mediterranean Fair (« la Fiera del Mediterraneo ») serves as a sort of gangway to Italy.

The Castle. - The central part of the castle was built by the emperor Frederick II in 1233, using the foundations of fortifications erected previously by the Normans during their long domination of the region. The ramparts, added at the beginning of the 16th century, are an early example of this structure used as a defence against artillery attacks. In the same period, the interior of the castle was modernised so as to serve as the residence of the duchesses Isabella of Aragon and Bona Sforza.

Basilica of San Nicola. - Built between 1087 and 1108 under the direction of the Benedictine monk Elias, the basilica is a prototype of the churches built in the region after the beginning of its period under Norman rule. It stands on the site of the previous residential palace of the « Capatano », the city's Greek governor during the 9th and 10th centuries, and the four open areas which still surround it today are known as the « courts of the Capatano ». The church is in the Apulian Romanesque style, though there are clear Byzantine influences. The fine central portal of the facade, with its door-posts by the so-called Como masters Ansaldo and Taddeo, with two columns on both sides, goes back to the 12th century. Beside the church are the two bell-towers which have been reduced in height because they were in danger of collapsing.

Panorama. - A distinct contrast can be seen between the two parts of the city: the old part, with its narrow alleys and houses without windows which seem to cling to the sides of the castle built by Frederick II; and the modern part, constructed according to advanced concepts of town planning with wide, parallel streets.

CASTEL DEL MONTE. - This is the finest and without doubt the most famous building in Apulia. It stands on the top of a hill 1750 feet high and thus dominates much of the Murge region. A structure of Swabian origin, it is predominantly Gothic in style but also has clearly Romanesque elements; its plan is octagonal and it has an octagonal tower standing at each angle. It was built in about 1240 by the Swabian emperor Frederick II as a hunting castle and filled with superb artistic works, though it was soon to become a gloomy dungeon. It passed into the hands of several families, the Acciaiuoli, Del Balzo and Carafa, and alternated between periods of splendour and of grim service as a police and military prison. Towards the middle of the 18th century, there was a period of serious pillaging in which valuable materials, including marble, columns and mosaics, disappeared. Only in 1876, when the Italian Government acquired the castle from the Carafa family, was restoration of this important building begun.

TRANI. The Cathedral. - During the Crusades, Apulia was a region of considerable importance because it was the point from which the ships left, sailing to the Holy Land, and to which they returned. This is why the art of Apulia at the time of the Crusades absorbed so many elements from different cultures. The Cathedral of Trani, dedicated to San Corrado, is a typical example. In it can be seen a mixture of stylistic influences, from the French features particularly evident in the facade to clearly Byzantine elements such as the mosaics inside the church.

ALBEROBELLO. Street with trulli. - A group of these typical Apulian buildings. The trullo is a structure with a centralised plan, which has a cone-shaped vault built up from stones laid without the use of mortar or cement. Its design is very ancient — it probably goes back to thousands of years before Christ — and it was brought to southern Italy by immigrants from Asia Minor. As a residence, the inside of the trullo has a central room, divided horizontally so as to provide an upper floor, and smaller rooms in the angles for cooking or other purposes.

LECCE. Church of Santa Croce. Detail. - The large rose-window in the church's facade, with its profuse decoration, is another example of the Baroque style, which achieved moments of considerable splendour in Apulia. The church, which is the finest in the city, was built in 1353 by order of Walter of Brienne, Duke of Athens, but its present-day appearance is the result of later works carried out between 1550 and 1700 by Gabriele Riccardo, Francesco Zimbolo and Cesare Penna.

BASILICATA

The present-day Basilicata, which includes the provinces of Potenza and Matera, is also commonly referred to as Lucania. The name Lucania derives from its prehistoric people, the Lyki. The Government has now reconfirmed Basilicata as the region's official name; it derives from the 11th-century Byzantine governor, the *basilikos*. In early times Greek settlers brought to the region their culture, art and philosophy (among the illustrious Greeks who came here were Pythagoras and Parmenides). The Lucanians, after a long war with Taranto, later became allies with Rome during the Samnite wars but then they too found themselves at war with Rome, and after 272 B.C. the Lucanian cities of Pandosia and Poseidonia became Roman colonies. The Lucanians sought to rebel against Rome but the Romans reacted with bloody repressions, and the region, which up until then had known periods of considerable splendour, was depopulated and deserted. Its decadence thus dates back to the 3rd century. In the 13th century cultural and artistic centres flourished briefly in the region, where the court of the Swabian emperor Frederick II made frequent sojourns. After his death and the brief stay in Italy of his ill-fated grandson Corradino, Potenza and other cities rose against the Angevin rulers, but with disastrous consequences. Basilicata was then left to itself in the most complete abandon. Life here between the 14th and 17th centuries was marked by continual struggles by the lower classes against the feudal barons and the governing authorities for possession of the land, the only asset sought after in all ranks of society.

In the 18th and 19th centuries the ruling classes remained deaf to the demands of the peasants. The lower classes of Basilicata were reduced to such misery that many turned to banditry; nor did the often bloody repression of the outlaws contribute in any way to the solution of the region's problems. Only since World War Two have land reforms begun to break up the large holdings, and Basilicata remains Italy's poorest and most backward region.

MATERA

For centuries the name of Matera has been linked with the areas known as the Sassi: two valleys where until recently, in cave-like dwellings hollowed out of the steep rock-faces, its peasants and craftsmen had lived for thousands of years. The inhabitants have now been moved elsewhere; but the Sassi remain as a reminder of the great difficulties which Matera has had to confront. In fact the Sassi have become something of a symbol of the conditions of the peasant class in southern Italy, conditions which have led to the unqualified commitment of the Italian Government to solve the « problem of the Mezzogiorno », as southern Italy is called. Matera has now been completely restructured under a town-planning scheme to which Italy's most important architects and planners, from Quaroni to Piccinato, have contributed. However, the inhabitants of the Sassi were transferred from their strange hovels without being offered a real possibility of economic integration, and this may well have created a more serious imbalance than that which existed previously. It is clearly not enough to move craftsmen, peasants and farm workers into new houses without first having radically transformed the structure of their economy. Convincing evidence of this is given by the village of La Martella, where the tenants of new houses still live on the most miserable incomes, aided by contributions from workers who have emigrated elsewhere. The history of the region's art is also obviously related to the kind of land in which its people live. Unique in all Italy, for example, are its cliff-side churches, buildings which are part of the earth itself and in which what are geologically caves have been transformed with Oriental motifs deriving from Byzantine influences. The most important of these is the Cathedral, built between 1268 and 1270 in the Apulian Romanesque style, its exterior preserving, with few alterations, the original form. Other churches of considerable interest are those of San Giovanni Battista, built in 1204, San Francesco, rebuilt in the Baroque style in 1670, and the Chiesa del Purgatorio, built in 1747.

Matera. - Panorama.

CALABRIA

Little is known of the history of Calabria until the 8th century B.C. when a series of colonies was founded by Greek settlers along the Ionic coast. This colonisation can be considered the beginning of the region's history. The first colonies established were Sybaris and Crotone, which were agricultural settlements rather than trading centres as might be expected. Other colonies followed: Reggio, Metaurum (the present-day Gioia Tauro) and Locris. Up until the end of the 7th century, Sybaris imposed its political authority on the other cities, though cultural leadership in the region belonged to Crotone. War broke out between the settlements and ended in 510 B.C. with the defeat and total destruction of Sybaris. Crotone dominated the region briefly, but when this city too fell into decline none of the other cities was sufficiently powerful to assert itself, and their independence was seriously menaced. In fact, the region came under the rule of the Sicilian city of Syracuse, at the same time feeling the pressure from the north of the Brutii, a people of Italic stock in central southern Italy. The invasions of the Visigoths, the long Gothic wars and the peasants' revolts plunged Calabria deeper and deeper into poverty. Between the 6th and 9th centuries the Longobards took possession of part of the region, while the remainder was controlled by the Sicilian aristocracy. When the Normans came in 1052 they encountered little resistance from the then Byzantine rulers and easily conquered the region, bringing with them the feudal system. There was a period of economic revival during the rule of the Swabian emperors, particularly under Frederick II, but after his death Calabria came under the Angevins and Aragonese and entered a phase of decadence which lasted until the 17th century. In the 18th century, rule passed into the hands of the Bourbons, without substantially changing conditions in the region. Only at the beginning of the 19th century was there a real resurgence: the feudal system was abolished, although the ruling classes gained if anything an increasing control of the land. What followed is recent history: Calabria took part in the Italian Risorgimento, fighting the same battles which were fought all over southern Italy to gain freedom from the Bourbon government and achieve unification with the rest of Italy. In Calabria today, undeniable progress has been made in many sectors, including the field of culture, though it is not exempt from the problem which plagues most of southern Italy, that of the migrant workers who must travel to northern Italy, Switzerland and Germany to find employment.

Reggio Calabria. National Museum. - *Clay group.* This superb group modelled in clay adorned the pediment of the Temple of Casa Marafioti at Locri. A work of remarkable interest and unique in its kind, it can be dated to the 5th century B.C.

REGGIO CALABRIA

Standing at the base of the rugged Aspromonte mountains, facing the Strait of Messina which has always promised it so much prosperity and brought it so many tribulations, Reggio Calabria today stands in more urgent need than ever of the long-promised bridge which will unite it with Sicily and finally strengthen the close ties it has had ever since ancient times with nearby Messina. Founded by the Greeks in the 8th century B.C., Reggio became a flourishing and prosperous city, but the visitor today will seek in vain for evidence of its past glories. Since 91 B.C., the city has been repeatedly devastated by earthquakes which have demolished its buildings time and time again. The last two above all, in 1783 and 1908, had catastrophic effects: the one on 28 December 1908 claimed no less than 8000 victims and destroyed most of the residential areas. Such constant adversities, plus the unyielding nature of the Calabrian earth, have created a people who are all too familiar with sorrow from their day of birth. But the very bitterness of the ordeal which the Calabrian must face in his arduous land often excites the admiration of people who live far away in the great cities. Reggio Calabria also offers the visitor beaches which are not yet crowded or polluted, the massive splendour of the Aspromonte mountains, and the beautiful specimens of Greek art in its National Museum.

Reggio Calabria. - On the left: a view of the seaside boulevard and the Strait of Messina, on the other side of which is the bluish brown mass of Sicily. On the right: the Duomo, a work by Father Carmelo Angioini which testifies to the astonishing resolution with which the entire city went about the task of rebuilding after the earthquake of 1908. Clearly to be seen in the church are elements inspired by Romanesque, Gothic and Renaissance styles.

CATANZARO. The City. - Standing 1100 feet above sea level, at the narrowest point in the whole Italian peninsula — the Tyrrhenian and Ionic Seas here are little more than twenty miles apart — Catanzaro was founded towards the end of the 9th century. Its history is part of that of the Neapolitan kingdom. The harsh soil, crossed by broad streams, has never permitted great agricultural development, and this has led to large-scale emigration.

COSENZA. - Founded by the Bruttii, a local Italic people, at the point where the Basento and Crati rivers meet, Cosenza was influenced by the Greek civilisation, although it remained independent until the year 204 B.C. when it was occupied by the Romans. According to a popular legend, Alaric, King of the Ostrogoths, died in the vicinity of the city in the year 410, and was buried in the bed of the river, temporarily diverted for the purpose. Buried with the king, the story goes, was the treasure he had plundered from Rome a few months before.

SICILY

According to historical tradition, the prehistoric inhabitants of the island of Sicily were the Siculi who had come from the Italian mainland, the Sicani who had come from Spain, and the Elimi, a mixed group of refugees from Lybia. Then the Greeks arrived and began founding their first colonies, at Catania and Lentini, and later, around 629 B.C., at Selinunte. The colonisation by the Greeks was virtually completed in the first half of the 6th century B.C. Syracuse became by far the most important city on the island, so that its history during the 6th, 5th and 4th centuries B.C. is virtually the history of Sicily. In the 5th century Syracuse's famous tyrant, Gelo, had to withstand repeated attacks on the island by the Phoenicians, attacks which were to last until the Carthaginian wars during the 3rd century B.C. With the help of the people of Imera and Agrigento, Gelo defeated the Carthaginian general Hamilcar, and six years later overcame the Etruscans at Cumae. The conflicts in Greece between the Doric and Attic cities also had repercussions for Syracuse, which was of Doric origin. In 409, the Carthaginian general Hannibal went to war against Syracuse, by now mistress of the whole of Sicily; Hannibal conquered Selinunte, Agrigento and Gela, but was unable to break down the resistance of Syracuse itself. It was left to Rome to put an end to the oscillating fortunes of these wars, and in 264 B.C. the Romans gained a foothold in Sicily. But the Roman conquest of the island did not become effective until 212 B.C. when, after a siege lasting more than two years, the consul Claudius Marcellus captured Syracuse. In Sicily, as in other regions under the dominion of Rome, rebellions broke out, first among the slaves and later among the peasants. Cities such as Syracuse, Gela and Agrigento, which had known periods of splendour, fell into decline while cities like Catania and Tindari entered a new phase of prosperity: thus the prosperous coastal zones stood in contrast with the backward areas in the interior.

After the decline of Roman power, Sicily was invaded first by the Vandals under Genseric, then by the Goths of Theodoric, and finally by the Byzantines who, under the command of Belisarius, took possession of the island where they were to remain for three cent-uries. At the end of this period, the Arabs challenged the Byzantine supremacy, and in 902, after no less than seventy-five years of fighting, gained control of the island. Compared with Byzantine rule, the Arab domination was without doubt a step forward for Sicily: under their enlightened government, it became an important centre of civilisation during the dark years when the Italian mainland suffered under the yoke of feudalism. In 1091, the Normans became its new rulers, and in the first half of the 12th century their kingdom extended from Naples to Sicily, with its capital in the Sicilian city of Palermo. Under the emperor Frederick II, Palermo grew to be one of the most advanced centres of art and learning in the world, but its stature declined suddenly with the transference of the capital to Naples. The Angevin policy was to introduce their characteristic feudal system, which acted to the exclusive advantage of the French rural aristocracy, and this situation led to the Vespri revolt in 1282, after which the Spaniard Pietro of Aragon was acclaimed as the island's new king. The Spaniards remained in Sicily until 1712, when it passed into the hands of Piedmont; later it came under Austrian rule, until it passed yet again from the Austrians to the Bourbon kings of Naples. None of these successive foreign rulers brought about a single improvement in the island's extremely backward conditions. Its resurgence did not begin until 1848, the year of rebellions throughout Europe, and later still it had a key part in the events of the Italian Risorgimento leading to its eventual union with the Kingdom of Italy. Only on 15 May 1946 was legislation passed granting Sicily administrative autonomy and beginning the process of cultural renovation for which the island had had to wait so many centuries.

PALERMO

Protected from behind by Mount Pellegrino, the city of Palermo looks out onto its vast gulf, which extends as far as Cape Zafferano. Obviously, from the time of its origins (which go back to the Phoenicians) the city's life has been linked to the sea. Today, if one wanders through the dingy little streets around the port, one comes face to face with the extreme poverty of the fishermen here who work incessantly and often manage only to satisfy their most basic needs. Of course, not far away to the north of this zone is the evidence of the new Palermo: new wharves, new jetties and new dykes. But the city's most interesting feature is the history of its art. From this point of view, the first aspect which comes to mind is its period of domination by the Arabs and the cultural and artistic heritage which they left, such as the three hundred mosques which were destroyed under the later Norman rule. And yet, through the extremely high level of culture which it attained, the Norman court was able to filter intelligently and assimilate the fruits of architectural, literary and poetic experiences which came to Palermo from the most diverse and far-flung sources: from England and Africa, from the East and from the other parts of Italy. When the influence of the Arab culture began its slow but inevitable decline, the Byzantine artistic tradition took its place. It continued to be important in the brilliant Swabian court of Frederick II, who made his capital at Palermo, giving birth to the famous Sicilian school of poets, Dante's predecessors. The foreign influences on Sicily's art and literature have always been successfully assimilated. This aspect of Sicily's culture, difficult to define but easily recognised, still survives today. It survives too in the character of the Sicilian people, proud but fearful, sometimes perhaps rather closed, but always ready to open up and smile. Here contrasts seem sharper, and problems seem more difficult and more dramatic. Here modern ways of life exist alongside archaic traditions and customs which belong to the feudal age; on the one hand, the glossy signs of progress, on the other the unequivocal evidence of misery which, though sometimes colourful and noisy, is never denied but rather accepted with resigned submission.

Palazzo dei Normanni. - Built and extended over a long period by the Norman kings, the palace stands on the site of a primitive Arab fortress. It was added to in succeeding periods, its present form being the result of extensions made during the 17th century, and became a luxurious royal palace and cultural centre.

Cloister of the church of San Giovanni degli Eremiti. - The typical little red domes of this church stand out against the sky, above the exuberant foliage of the vegetation at its base. Built by order of Ruggero II in 1132, it is a fine example of the Arabo-Norman style. The splendid cloister is a later addition, but its twin columns supporting pointed arches combine happily with the earlier structure.

MONREALE

Interior of the Duomo. - The Cathedral was built around 1176 by Guglielmo II and was extended in the 16th and 17th centuries, without however disfiguring its beauty; in fact is is generally considered the finest Norman church in Sicily. The interior, notable for its rich golden decorative motifs, is divided into three naves with three apses. The lower part of the walls is dressed with marble, and on the upper part is a mosaic cycle recounting the history of the Christian religion.

Cloister of the Duomo. - It is difficult to add anything to the praise already lavished on this oasis of peace and serenity. Part of the ancient Benedictine monastery, the cloister is surrounded by 216 twin columns which support the arches of its portico and which have capitals sculpted in the most various and imaginative forms.

SEGESTA. The theatre. - Cut out of a rocky hillside, the theatre commands a magnificent panorama, in which the gulf of Castellamare, Alcamo, Partinico and Montelepre can be clearly seen. Segesta was founded in about the 12th century B.C. and was essentially Greek in character. It was a bitter enemy of Selinunte and succeeded in overwhelming that city with the help of the Carthaginians. But it was the rule of the Carthaginians which most weakened Segesta, and around the 10th century the Vandals and Saracens destroyed it completely.

SELINUNTE. Remains of Temple C. - Founded by Greek settlers, probably in 628 B.C., Selinunte reached a high level of development, and its grandeur can still be appreciated today from the ruins of its monuments. Selinunte was frequently at war with the neighbouring city of Segesta, and it was during one of these battles, in the year 409 B.C., that the city was destroyed by the Carthaginians, fighting on the side of Segesta. Its temples, whose exact function is uncertain, are indicated by letters of the alphabet (Temple A, Temple B, etc.), and the one shown in the photo is the most ancient and the largest in the Acropolis.

AGRIGENTO. Temple of Concordia. - Built in the first half of the 5th century B.C., this is the best conserved of the many Greek temples to be found in the celebrated « Valley of the Temples » with its gently sloping hills near Agrigento. Its present name derives from a Latin inscription found in the vicinity, but has no connection with the temple's original function which remains unknown.

SYRACUSE. Roman amphitheatre. - Built at the time of Augustus, it is elliptical in form, and is partly carved out of the rock and partly built in masonry.

SARDINIA

Sardinia, the second biggest island after Sicily in the Mediterranean, has remained isolated for many centuries from the cultural and political progress achieved on the Italian mainland. Originally, it was populated by peoples from various origins: settlers came here from Africa, Spain, Liguria and Corsica. An important step in the social structure of the island took place in prehistoric times when, for defence reasons, the inhabitants of Sardinia began to build the castles known as « nuraghi »: these were round towers, shaped like the base of a cone and built of stones held in place without the use of cement — the fortresses of the Bronze and Iron ages. In the 12th century B.C. the Phoenician ships which sailed towards Spain and Britain began using the island as a regular port of call, and established commercial centres of considerable importance. Four centuries later, maritime supremacy had passed from the Phoenicians to the Greeks, and Greek navigators sought to colonise the northern part of Sardinia, provoking an immediate reaction from the Etruscans and the Carthaginians. This sparked off a long war which resulted in the victory of the Carthaginians and withdrawal of the Sardinian people to the mountainous interior of the island. Thus two separate cultures were formed, the more advanced among the Carthaginian settlers along the coasts and the backward culture of the natives in the interior. The island had by now become both an important strategic base for the control of the Mediterranean and a fertile producer of cereal foods. This explains the Romans' desire to conquer it, and in fact, after their long, exhausting war against Carthage, Sardinia came under Roman rule. With the gradual spread of Roman civilisation, even the mountain peoples began to emerge from their isolation; like all foreign tribes, they had been called by the Romans « barbarians », from which derives the name of the present-day region of Barbagia.

After Rome's power had dwindled, Arab expansionism began, though the Arabs sacked and plundered Sardinia without trying to conquer it. In the period immediately after the year 1000 Sardinia became a bone of contention between the maritime republics of Pisa and Genoa, though the city of Cagliari remained mainly under Pisan control. The Pisan and Genoese interests wrought a transformation in the island: new trading prospects were opened up, and the cities of Sardinia became richer and more important. At the beginning of the 14th century, Sardinia became a possession of the Spanish kingdom of Aragon. Under Aragonese rule, feudalism was introduced to the island, marking the disappearance of the institutions derived from the free commune and brought here previously by Genoa and Pisa. Sardinia remained under Spanish control until the late 15th century, when the Spanish kingdoms of Aragon and Castile were unified, but this brought no relief to the island from the increasingly rapacious and unscrupulous exploitation by its Spanish viceroys. Under the Rastadt treaty of 1714, Sardinia came under the rule of Austria, which yielded it in turn to the House of Savoy in exchange for Sicily in 1720. The entire period of Savoy rule was one of efficient administration, which led to the repopulation of parts of the island and the settling of others, plus an increase in agricultural production and improved public services. However, the conversion from one economic system to another, which involved the abolition of feudal holdings, inevitably caused a crisis whose effects were felt above all by the peasants. The angry reaction to this found its outlet in isolated outbreaks of violence, which eventually degenerated into banditry. New interest was taken in Sardinia after the proclamation of the Kingdom of Italy in 1861, but the grave problems in its pastoral and agricultural sectors remained unsolved. After the Second World War, the island's Action Party demanded administrative autonomy for Sardinia, which was granted on 29 February 1948.

CAGLIARI

The first thing which strikes the visitor arriving in Cagliari by sea is the extraordinary contrast between the elegant modern street which is Via Roma and the popular zone which lies behind it. The fashionable doorways which line Via Roma give access to boutiques, chic cafes and modern offices, but behind this facade are winding alleyways which still have a somewhat Moorish aspect and the ancient houses in which the fishermen live. Cagliari, occupied by the Vandals and Goths, suffered innumerable attacks by the Arabs, was torn by the rivalry between Genoa and Pisa, ruled by the Aragonese, then for a long decade by Austria, and finally by the Savoys before its eventual independence. Its artistic history is equally complicated. The art of Pisa had a delayed influence but many years before 1257 when Pisa took possession of Cagliari the foundation had been laid for its Cathedral, in which the geometrical rigour still apparent in the sections of the walls and two architraves which remain clearly indicates the presence of artists from across the sea. Dating from the period under Spanish domination are the Church and Cloister of San Domenico, and the churches called the Chiesa della Speranza and Chiesa della Purissima. They are built in a less rigorous style, with more flexible forms, but nevertheless reveal an awareness of the Gothic advances. In fact, the classical forms were assimilated and translated into the local language, so that a style was created which became typical of the whole of Sardinia and which lasted as long as the Spaniards remained on the island. The Baroque forms underwent the same process. Under Piedmontese rule the rich Baroque style was replaced by the austere and rigorously simple style favoured by the Savoy rulers. Finally, after the unification of Italy, the face of the city of Cagliari was rapidly transformed as it kept pace with the latest architectural and town-planning advances on the mainland of Italy.

NEBIDA. The cliffs. - Another example of the variety of Sardinia's coastline. A comparison with the photo above reveals the profound difference in physical structure.

MURAVERA. The beach. - This enchanting and tranquil beach is on the eastern side of the island, near the mouth of the Flumendosa, Sardinia's second most important river. Behind it lie almond groves and citrus orchards.

BARUMINI. Nuraghe palace. - This is the main building of an entire village of « nuraghi » discovered in this place. The nuraghe is a conical construction made from blocks of stone laid without the use of mortar. Dating from the Bronze Age, the structure marks an important moment in the evolution of civilisation in Sardinia.

SASSARI. The Duomo. - Dedicated to San Nicola, the Cathedral was erected around 1480, though the redundant facade in imitation Spanish Baroque style was superimposed on it at the beginning of the 18th century. Sassari was probably founded in the Middle Ages: its ancient name, Thatari (still used today in the dialect of the region), begins to appear on maps in the 12th century.

ALGHERO. Portal of the Duomo. - The Cathedral, which is mentioned as far back as the 14th century, has been considerably rebuilt over the centuries. Of the original structure, only the Gothic-style portal and the bell-tower above it remain. The Alghero region was under the dominion of the Dorians in the 13th century B.C., though the origins of the city are not well known. In later times, it was ruled for many years by the Aragonese and a numerous Catalan colony was established here, leaving traces which can still be found in the local dialect today.

CAMPIDANO. - A typical view of the Sardinian countryside, with one of its characteristic nuraghi. The nuraghi were built for defensive purposes, and the entrance was often further protected by an enclosure. The large chamber inside is covered by a vault consisting of rings of ever-decreasing diameter laid one upon the other.